APPROPRIATE FOR AGES 8 THROUGH 108
PERFORMED BY GRADES 4 THROUGH 12, AND ADULTS, TOO!

# Peace Begins with You and Me

*A Musical Play with Life-Changing Messages
for Every Generation!*

A creative and educational resource for children that teaches
the positive power of our words, actions, feelings and thoughts.
Inspires anti-bullying, inclusion, nonviolence, empathy,
self-esteem, transformation and hope.

**Cheryl Melody Baskin**
**www.cherylmelody.com**

Copyright © 2020 by Cheryl Melody Baskin All Rights Reserved.

No part of this book may be reproduced or transmitted in any form or by any means, electronic or mechanical, including photocopying or recording. It may not be stored by any information storage and retrieval system or transmitted or copied for public or private use- other than for "fair use" as brief quotations embodied in articles and reviews. "Fair use" may be gained with written consent of the author.

All information provided within this book is for educational, informational and inspirational purposes only. It is not intended to diagnose or treat any illnesses or intended as a substitute for care from a professional. Please consult your physician or qualified health professional for diagnosis, advice, counseling and medical treatment. The intent of the author is to offer her personal insights and life experiences to guide children, parents and teachers. If you choose to use any of the information in this book, the author assumes no responsibility.

Library of Congress Cataloging-in-Publication Data Library of Congress Control Number: 2019920453 Baskin, Cheryl Melody Peace Begins with You and Me Cheryl Melody Baskin Paperback ISBN 978-1-7333681-2-4

Categories: *Children's Books *Bullying *Mental Health *Children's Emotions Books *Mindfulness *Character-Building Values *Performing Arts *Dramas and Musical Plays *Middle School Education *Elementary School Education *High School Education *Diversity *Growing Up and the Facts of Life *Child Psychology *Nonviolent Conflict-Resolution *Crisis Management Counseling *Creative Arts

ISBN 978-1-7333681-2-4

Library of Congress Control Number: 2019920453

© 2020

Cheryl Melody Baskin, LLC

*For all the children on our small precious planet ...*

# Contents

A Letter of Hope ............................................................................................................. 1

"Three Words" ................................................................................................................ 4

"Peace Begins with You and Me" — A Guide ............................................................... 5

Cast of Characters .......................................................................................................... 10

Act 1, Scene 1: Nine Amazing Kids .............................................................................. 14

Act 1, Scene 2: Life Lessons 101 ................................................................................... 16

Act 1, Scene 3: Kids Can Make a World of Difference ................................................. 24

Act 2, Scene 1: Peace is a Verb ...................................................................................... 30

Act 2, Scene 2: Peace Promises ..................................................................................... 35

Act 3, Scene 1: An Important Letter is Sent .................................................................. 40

Act 3, Scene 2: The Children's Dream — One Planet ................................................... 42

"Shift of Heart" .............................................................................................................. 47

About the Author ........................................................................................................... 48

Contact Information ....................................................................................................... 49

With a Grateful Heart .................................................................................................... 50

"Peace Begins with You and Me" Song Lyrics ............................................................. 51

Sheet Music .................................................................................................................... 63

# A Letter of Hope

Dear Beautiful Human Being and Teacher of Peace,

Thank you for choosing to perform *"Peace Begins with You and Me"* with your children. This consciousness-raising play is dedicated to instilling a sense of hope while teaching the core values of self-respect, respect for each other, caring for the earth, the prevention of bullying, anti-bias, inclusion, nonviolent conflict-resolution, effective dialogue and diversity celebration.

My name is Cheryl Melody Baskin, and I am the author of *"Peace Begins with You and Me."* Although I wrote this play to help create positive changes in our children, ourselves, each other and the planet, it has also helped to heal my own life. All the work that I have created as a playwright, author of two self-help books, educator, composer, recording artist and performer has served to diminish my own wounds from being a target of childhood bullying and religious prejudice. Whether I work with children or adults, my themes and intentions remain the same. I provide power words and messages that vibrate the essence of love, inclusion, inspiration, personal empowerment, healing, peace and hope.

The seed of *"Peace Begins with You and Me"* began in 2000 when I was introduced to Bob Silverstein, another peace educator and musician. He and his friend, Steve Diamond, had written a short but powerful story about children who learned that they could make a difference in the world. It was called, *"One Day in Peace."* As soon as I read the story, original music poured out of me, and after receiving permission from both Bob and Steve to expand their book, creative ideas began to fill my life. It didn't take long for me to realize that these important themes could become a meaningful musical play with the possibility of making a positive difference in children's lives all over the world. Soon, more songs were composed, and before I knew it, new albums were born. Each song was a seed and a possibility for inclusion into the peace play, and yet the albums, *"World Peace - The Children's Dream," "Celebrate"* and *"Friends Forever"* could stand independently, too. Since this musical could be changed and expanded at will, more and more songs became available for the *"Peace Begins with You and Me"* play, including two of Bob Silverstein's songs, *"Different and the Same"* and *"Kids Care."*

Although *"Peace Begins with You and Me"* has been revised many times, the messages remain the same. All children need peace, unconditional love, acceptance, inclusion, safety, stability, compassion and guidance, and after many years as an educator and a healing arts and creativity specialist, I know that the creative arts serve as a catalyst towards reaching and teaching the hearts and minds of children. Because of the high volume of school shootings, bullying, prejudice and drug addiction, I recently revised and updated this script once again.

**Behind-the-Scenes:** Over the years, teachers from all around the world have purchased *"Peace Begins with You and Me,"* and it is always amazing to me that the messages of the play are reverberating internationally. Not only has it been performed in the United States, but also in Africa, Canada, England, India, Philippines, South America, and beyond. Although I was delighted with the response to this meaningful play, I found myself envisioning an additional way to spread the concept of "being peace." As a result, *"Peace Begins with You and Me"* has had a life of its own.

Soon after the release of the children's play, I developed a live concert with the same name as the play, and performed it in public and private schools, churches, synagogues and for other organizations all around the United States. Some of the states included Florida, Hawaii, Massachusetts, Oklahoma, Pennsylvania, Rhode Island, Vermont and Virginia. My concert was interactive and required that the teachers prepare the children ahead of time. They did such a great job! When I arrived the children already knew the play's theme song, *"One Planet,"* listened to all the songs on the albums, *"Celebrate," "World Peace - The Children's Dream"* and *"Friends Forever,"* created individual "Peace Promises," and participated in many discussions on bullying, prejudice, and the power of our words and actions.

**9/11:** My first *"Peace Begins with You and Me"* concert was scheduled for a performance at a school in Boston, Massachusetts. The Sisters of St. Joseph received a grant to hire me to perform in many of their schools across the inner city, and the first concert was scheduled for September 12, 2001. A day before the concert, the way I had planned to present it shifted dramatically. On September 11, 2001, there was a terrorist attack on the World Trade Center in New York City. This traumatic event impacted everyone, including our precious and innocent children. Although the slogan, "the show must go on," was an emotional challenge for me, I knew that I needed to show up for the children, no matter what. When it was time for me to perform, I let go of my own agenda and created the time to listen to the children's feelings. During a time in which I myself felt great darkness, I used music and its powerful messages to give every student a sense of hope and empowerment. I'm not sure how I did it, but somehow I found the strength within me to offer the children light, love and compassion, and as a result, it helped to lift my own spirit, too. As I performed more concerts throughout the United States, my focus continued to be on providing hope and, as Gandhi said, to teach the children to "be the change they wish to see in the world."

Thank you for taking a positive part in the children's lives and inspiring them to walk the path of love, empathy and nonjudgment. By teaching and living the concept of "being peace," we embrace the responsibility and the honor of inspiring and elevating our children, ourselves and the planet. Peace truly does begin within each one of us by what we say, think, do and feel, and *"Peace Begins with You and Me"* can be a positive compass for *every* age, one beautiful person at a time.

I encourage you to breathe in trust, patience and a strong knowing that how you choose to implement the play will be just right. The main goals are to provide another path for communication and understanding, to help children know that they are not alone with their thoughts and feelings, and to give them additional tools for shifting their behavior. I leave you with the lyrics to a song I wrote called, "Three Words." Although I wrote it for adults, you may like the simple melody and message enough to use it in the play. The song is on an album entitled, *"Listen to the Whispers,"* and you can download the song from Amazon Music, Apple Music, CD Baby or iTunes. Enjoy the process, and always breathe in a megadose of hope, love and peace, no matter what.

From my heart to yours,

Cheryl Melody Baskin

## "Three Words"

### by Cheryl Melody

"Three Words" can be found on Amazon Music, Apple Music, CD Baby and iTunes. It is also part of an album entitled, *"Listen to the Whispers."*

Hope is the feeling to keep inside of you.
Love is the answer with our words and with what we do.
Peace is the vision we must imagine near,
Keep these three words in your heart clear.

Hope, love, peace is the way,
Hope, love, peace is the way.

If the world feels too heavy to bear in your soul,
And your heart is on empty and you feel far from whole.
If you're feeling angry, confused and alone,
Remember these three words to come home to yourself …
Remember these three words to come home.

Hope, love, peace is the way,
Hope, love, peace is the way.

*"Peace Begins with You and Me"*

# A Guide

**More than a Play:** *"Peace Begins with You and Me"* is more than a play. It is designed to help students, teachers and parents address challenging issues, and it serves as a seed that can lead to many value-oriented activities. Performing the *"Peace Begins with You and Me"* musical perfectly is not the main goal. The goal is to teach children how to work together in a cooperative and respectful environment. They also begin to understand the meaning of every word written in the script and how each word applies to their lives. Directors and teachers often set aside extra time to discuss various topics that may come up in the script, and these topics become the catalyst for voicing additional concerns.

Creative writing, discussion, journal writing, "Peace Promises" and *"Peace Begins with You and Me"* Clubs can also be integrated into the curriculum before, during and after school. Most of all, *"Peace Begins with You and Me"* becomes a message that has the power to influence children's choices and affect the trajectory of their lives.

**Editing and Duration:** *"Peace Begins with You and Me"* may be edited and interpreted freely without my permission. Because of this unique and flexible script, a definite duration for this play cannot be firmly indicated. The duration is dependent upon your own creative choices.

**Costumes, Props and Scenery:** The simplicity *or* the elaborate details of costumes, props and scenery will depend on your support network. They can be very basic and still be highly effective. All scenes take place in and around the school - the cafeteria, the classroom or outdoors.

**Creative Writing and Group Discussions:** To make this project meaningful for you and your students, there are many flexible options. If you find that the script needs to address specific problems in your school, teachers often integrate creative writing and discussions into their lessons, and then weave the children's thoughts and issues into the *"Peace Begins with You and Me"* script. As a result, children soon realize that they can become playwrights, too!

**Act I:** If your children are young, or rehearsal time is at a premium, many directors only perform Act I as a solution. Some directors allow children to read from the script; others encourage students to memorize all the words; some have elaborate sets; others use simple sets. Above all, I encourage you to make this play your own and use it as a steppingstone towards raising awareness about the power of our words, thoughts, feelings and actions.

**Characters:** The characters in this play are not described in detail, and when they are described specifically, this too can be freely altered to suit your needs. Feel free to add, modify or delete any characters, words and songs. If there is someone who can integrate sign language, please add it to the play, and any children who have special needs should always be represented. In addition, there are non-speaking roles which allow for a wide variety of ages, preferences and personalities, and adults are often part of the *"Peace*

*Begins with You and Me"* experience, too. Above all, since this play is meant to embrace an inclusive philosophy, please find a creative way to integrate different cultures.

**Narrators:** The narrators are not only telling the story, but they are also listening and reacting *to* the story. The parts are lengthy. You may want to divide the narrator parts among several children, ask a few adults to assume the role, or invite children to read the words, rather than memorizing them.

**"One Planet:"** The song, *"One Planet,"* is the theme song of the play, and it can be sung at the beginning and at the end of the story. To download it, search for the name "Cheryl Melody" on Amazon Music, Apple Music, CD Baby or iTunes. *"One Planet"* can also be found on the albums, *"Celebrate," "World Peace - The Children's Dream"* and *"Friends Forever."* The full notation/transcription of *"One Planet"* accompanies your script, and there is also a video featuring this song ...

https://www.youtube.com/watch?v=ClvTg7rmn0o

**Additional Songs and Lyrics:** In addition to choosing familiar songs with themes of inclusion, love and kindness, I have also written many songs that will enhance the meaning of the *"Peace Begins with You and Me"* experience. All songs can be found on the albums *"Celebrate," "Friends Forever"* and *"World Peace - The Children's Dream."* You may also want to use a beautiful song called *"Wishes"* from the album, *"Songs That Make the Heart Feel Good,"* and you can find this song on Amazon Music, Apple Music, CD Baby or iTunes.

Every word in every song contains messages of what "being peace" means, and all songs are written in easy keys and teachable. First, listen to the many sound samples from each of my albums online, discerning which songs feel right for your situation. If the children are young, choose songs that contain simple lyrics, melodies and rhythms. If they are older, choose more sophisticated songs.

Although I have enclosed the notation for seven songs, adapt the melodies and rhythms to your needs. If you feel that an additional song should be put in a different section of the script, insert it. If you prefer a different song than the one suggested, believe in your idea. Once your music is chosen and downloaded, children could also sing with my voice as their guide.

## Musical Recommendations

**"*Celebrate*" album:**

*"One Planet," "Mother Earth," "Shake Your Own Hand," "Stand Proud," "You Can Change You," "Peace is a Verb," "The No Bully Rap - Song," "Piece or Peace - A Seriously Silly Spelling Song," "Kids Can Make a World of Difference," "If You Have a Dream"*

**"*Friends Forever*" album:**

*"Give Friendship a Chance," "The Smile of Friendship," "Friends Forever"*

**"*World Peace - The Children's Dream*" album:**

*"Different and the Same," "Kids Care," "Peaceful Warrior Dance," "World Peace Anthem," "Mother Earth, Father Sky," "The Children's Dream," "One Day in Peace"*

**"*Songs That Make the Heart Feel Good*" album:**

*"The Friendship Song," "Wishes"*

**Where can this music be purchased?** All songs can be heard as sound samples and then downloaded. They are under the name, *"Cheryl Melody,"* and are available on Amazon Music, Apple Music, CD Baby and iTunes.

**A Note to the Director:** In the script, you will discover a bonus rap/chant called, *"Earth Rap."*

**Earth Chorus:** Although the entire cast can be part of the Earth Chorus, you could also have a separate Earth Chorus. Your decision depends upon the number of children involved in your cast as a whole.

**Earth Band:** Enjoy adding rhythm instruments for the chorus section in "Peace is a Verb" and the chorus section of "Earth Rap."

**Adults:** Although it is optional, there are many opportunities for adults to participate in the *"Peace Begins with You and Me"* play.

**Audience:** There are participatory opportunities for the audience to react to the *"Peace Begins with You and Me"* experience.

## Peace Promises - A Teaching Tool

**Creating a Peace Buzz:** One of the most important tools for reinforcing the messages of this play is an experiential approach called "Peace Promises." These promises can be created during the "*Peace Begins with You and Me*" process, and their formation involves inner reflection, creative writing, verbal sharing and personal transformation. In fact, peace promises can be an effective approach for creating a "peace buzz" throughout the entire school. Even children who are not part of the cast can participate. To create a heightened vibration of "being peace," children could place their "*Peace Begins with You and Me*" promises, artwork, essays, poems, raps, songs and murals throughout the entire school.

They could also reflect and respond to the following questions: *Did your words and actions show respect for yourself and for the other person? Did you give people who were different from you a chance? Did you listen to another person's point of view? Were you more understanding and caring? What are your "Peace Begins with You and Me" examples? Have you changed for the better in any way? Are you a positive role model? How does it feel?*

**Positive Transformation:** Through the Peace Promise activity, the transformation in children is often palatable. In fact, I have witnessed miracles! Many children who were known as the bullies in the school created promises that reflected a heightened sensitivity to the emotional damage that their bullying caused in others. Some of these students even had the courage to stand up in front of the audience and share their new positive intentions!

**Peace Promises:** Over the years, I have been honored to hear children and adults create powerful Peace Promises …

## My Peace Promise

Ashley: *I promise to be a good example to others, stand up for others, be kind, never use violence, and be kind to my mom and my brother.*

Travis: *I promise to think before I speak, and not bully or call people names. I promise to be kind to everyone and not harm them.*

Gloria: *I promise not to take drugs like my brother does, and I promise to take care of my body.*

Mitchell: *I promise to always tell the truth.*

Hannah: *I promise to love everyone, share with others, forgive others, and not fight.*

Dustin: *I promise to be polite and not kick others, do kind things, and not listen when kids say unkind words.*

Kendall: *I promise not to embarrass other kids. I promise to help friends and other people.*

Erin: *I promise to compliment others and not act like a bully. I promise to be kind to my sister at all times.*

Mara: *I promise to comfort someone when they are hurt or sad, speak kind words to others, not call names, and help others when in need.*

Taylor: *I promise to respect my mom by not yelling at her, and I promise to be a good example for my new baby sister.*

Brandi: *I promise to help poor people have a home by working with my city. I promise to help a friend when she or he gets hurt.*

Kari: *I promise to forgive and not fight with other kids. I promise to be patient with my classmates and not call them names.*

Simon: *I promise to help people who are in trouble.*

Matthew: *I promise to help spread peace around the world by talking and listening to people.*

Emma: *I promise to clean up my room and wash the dishes with my mother.*

Madeline: *I promise to help feed hungry people by doing chores to raise money to buy food.*

Kristen: *I promise to talk and listen to people I disagree with.*

Fiona: *I promise not to be bad, and I won't fight with my brothers.*

Peyton: *I promise to help keep the earth clean so it will be a peaceful place to live.*

Helen: *I promise to be friends with everybody.*

Eugene: *I promise to love my family and to help everyone.*

Elijah: *I promise to help my mom with everything she needs.*

Lauren: *I promise to help people and be nice to my friends.*

Jennifer: *I promise to be nice to my sisters.*

Liam: *I promise to work for peace by being a good role model.*

## Cast of Characters

*"Peace Begins with You and Me"* unfolds into a musical story about children from all backgrounds who learn how to respect themselves and each other. As their transformation and awareness grows, they discover innovative ways to invite support so that the true meaning of "being peace" becomes a unified vision for every school, home and neighborhood throughout the whole world.

**Narrator 1**

**Narrator 2** (*choose more narrators, if needed*)

**Primary Cast:** (*nine kids with an amazing idea*)

Rosa

Maya

Shamice

WeiLing

Johnny

Amani

David

Mohammed

Jason

**The Bullies:** (*who eventually change for the better*)

Georgie

Luther

Chuck

Daphne

Gloria

**Other Students:** (*Peace Promises*)

Eva

Daniel

Emily

Jeremy

Other Children (*Peace Promises and non-speaking roles*)

**Reader:** "To the People of the World"

**Teachers:**

Mrs. Rosen

Mr. King

Mr. Casey

Mrs. Burgette

Other Teachers (*Peace Promises and non-speaking roles*)

**Parents:**

Mr. Jackson

Mrs. Patel

Mr. Goldberg

Mrs. Kelly

Mr. Campbell

Other Parents/Grandparents (*Peace Promises and non-speaking roles*)

**Earth Chorus**

**Earth Band** (*shakers, drums, world instruments, or any basic rhythm instruments*)

**Audience** (*interactive*)

**A Note to the Director-Casting**: The roles in the "*Peace Begins with You and Me*" play can be reduced or expanded. Choices will depend on your circumstances. If you do not have an adequate number of people to support each role in the script, feel free to delete parts. For example, if the script calls for five parents, you could narrow the roles to just one or two parents, and if it calls for five teachers, you could change the script to include only one or two teachers. Besides the 14 children in the main cast of characters, (*six girls and eight boys*), there are also four additional children (*two girls and two boys*), and nonspeaking roles as well. If you have a small group, eliminate the roles for the extra children, and even delete some of the primary roles. The Earth Chorus can comprise of children who do not have speaking parts, or you can integrate the entire cast. The sky is the limit. *No matter what changes you decide to make, this play will be flexible enough to still convey its meaningful messages.*

# Peace Begins with You and Me

*A Musical Play with Life-Changing Messages for Every Generation!*

By Cheryl Melody Baskin

## Act 1, Scene 1

## Nine Amazing Kids

> **A Note to the Director - Suggestion**: Choose character-building topics that pertain to your group of children and feel free to write these issues into the script.

**Scene:** Outdoors. Everyone is talking and playing. As the narrators come forward to tell the story to the audience, the kids notice that the narrators are talking about them.

**Narrator 1:** *(talks to the audience)* Thank you for joining us. We'd like to tell you a story about kids who made something amazing happen. *(gestures to the children nearby)* These kids. Now, before we tell you about the powerful actions they created together, first let me say that these kids did *not* always get along.

**Narrator 2:** *(nods in agreement)* That's right. They used to tease each other for all kinds of reasons - skin color, the clothes they wore, different religions, disabilities …

**Narrator 1:** Or for being too tall, too short, too fat, too skinny, too smart, not smart enough, too rich, too poor, too shy, too loud, too quiet … I mean it was awful! All they did was put each other down!

*(the kids overhear the narrators)*

**Mohammed:** *(turns to his friends)* That's right. It *was* awful! I just moved here from another country and I didn't speak much English. Some of you weren't nice to me at all. You didn't include me in *anything*, *(looks hurt and shakes head)* and I got teased *all* the time.

**WeiLing:** I'm sorry that happened to you, Mohammed. This won't make you feel any better, but *I* had a hard time when *I* moved here, too. Most of you didn't want to come over to my house … and I felt *so* alone.

**Rosa:** That's awful, WeiLing. It's no excuse, but I guess we were *all* going through different situations. In my case, I felt too *embarrassed* to ask any of you to come over and meet my family. They just fight all the time, and some of them have serious drug addictions. To be honest, I would pick fights with you so you *wouldn't* like me … and you wouldn't *want* to come over to my house.

**David:** I feel so *bad* hearing all this. In *my* family, our religious customs are very different than yours. I was afraid I'd be called names if you knew. Besides, I really didn't know *how* to be included … and *still* be *me*.

**Amani:** This is so sad. In my situation, *none* of you talked to me at first. You didn't know what to do with a blind guy, I guess.

**Maya:** *That's* not true, Amani. I liked you right away! I just didn't know what I should do to make you feel more comfortable. *(frowns)* You know what, everybody? I had a hard time, too. Most of you didn't even give me a *chance* to be your friend. *(feels hurt)* I'm not even sure why to this day!

**Shamice:** I don't know why that happened either, Maya. You're so nice! As for me, I *know* I had a chip on my shoulder at first. I didn't think you would even *give* me a chance. I experienced so much prejudice and name-calling in my old school, I just thought you were all going to be the same way to me.

**Johnny:** *(guarded)* Yeah, I get what you're saying, Shamice. I kept to myself for some of the same reasons. I just thought it was *better* that way.

**Jason:** Well, it wasn't better, Johnny. We *wanted* to get to know you.

**Johnny:** Thanks, Jason. *(smiles)* I've been feeling a lot more comfortable these days.

**Jason:** That's good, Johnny. Hey, you guys. I don't know if you remember, but I used to be *very* shy. If you didn't talk to me, I didn't talk to you. I just stuck to myself and did my thing. *(smiles)* Now I feel *so* comfortable, you can't keep me *quiet*, right? *(the kids laugh)*

**Maya:** We sure *can't* keep you quiet, Jason, and I'm glad you're talking to us now. Besides, I like a lot of your ideas and the way you speak up about different issues.

**Jason:** Thanks, Maya. That makes me feel confident enough to share my ideas even more!

**WeiLing:** I agree with Maya, Jason. You know … it's so much better between *all* of us these days. *(kids agree)* If we keep treating each other like this, it's gonna be more and more fun around here every day! *(everyone agrees)*

---

**Song Suggestions:** "One Planet" from "Celebrate," or download "Friends Forever" from the album, "Friends Forever"

---

**Curtain Closes**

## Act 1, Scene 2

# Life Lessons 101

> **A Note to the Director:** If the following section feels inaccurate for your individual school issues, please modify the script. Encourage the children to create their own dialogue as a creative writing lesson and a discussion catalyst. Integrate their ideas and concerns into the following section, emphasizing what is true for *your* population. What are the children going through in your school, in their families and in their neighborhoods?

**Scene:** Cafeteria (Lunchroom; Cafetorium)

**Narrator I:** While most kids were respectful to each other now, there were some kids who *still* had important lessons to learn …

**Narrator II:** Let's listen in …

**WeiLing:** Hi. Is this seat taken?

**Chuck:** This spot isn't taken, but it's *not* for someone like *you*.

**Gloria:** No way.

**Luther:** Go sit somewhere else.

**Georgie:** This is reserved for *normal* kids.

**Daphne:** The *other* table is over *there*.

*(WeiLing walks to the other table with her head down, feeling sad and hurt. Jason and his friends are sitting at a different table and notice what is happening to her)*

**Jason:** Hey, WeiLing. Don't sit alone.

**Shamice**: Come sit with us. (*WeiLing walks over to their table with a relieved smile*)

**Maya:** Don't let them bother you, WeiLing.

**Johnny:** They're just bullies.

**Amani:** They just like to see if you will react and feel hurt.

**Rosa:** Besides, they don't know what they're *missing* by not including you.

**David:** *We* know how nice you are.

**Mohammed:** We would *never* treat you like that. (*smiles*) Stick with us.

**WeiLing:** (*smiles*) Okay. Thanks everybody. You just made me feel *so* much better.

**Narrator 1:** Suddenly they notice Georgie, Luther, Chuck, Gloria and Daphne fighting with each *other* …

**Narrator 2:** This seems bad …

**Georgie:** Don't mess with me, you guys!

**Luther and Chuck:** Ooo, we're soo scared. (*mocking him*)

**Gloria**: Don't you mess with *me,* either.

**Daphne:** (*speaks to Gloria*) Hey, quit pushing.

**Gloria:** *You* quit pushing *me*.

**Daphne:** (*Daphne notices Jason and his friends watching them*) What are *you* all looking at? You better be careful, or we'll come after *you*, too.

**Luther:** (*threatens them*) Ya, watch out.

**Jason:** (*yells over to them*) Why don't you just stop fighting with each other, stop bugging WeiLing and stop threatening *us*? Just be friendly. It's not that hard.

**Georgie:** No way!

**Luther:** Are you kidding?

**Daphne:** Be friends with *you*?

**Chuck:** We don't have one thing in common with you.

**Gloria:** Ya, not one single thing.

**Jason:** Really? I bet that not's true. You're the ones that are missing out.

**Mohammed:** (*Mohammed feels overwhelmed and confides in his friends*) You know what? This situation makes me feel *so* uncomfortable. They even *cyberbully* me online. I think we should talk to the teachers. Our parents, too. Maybe *they* have some ideas about how to handle all this.

**Rosa:** Mohammed is right.

**Amani:** *I* can't stand it anymore either.

**Johnny:** Maybe our teachers and parents *can* help us.

**David:** This is more than we can deal with ourselves, that's for sure!

**Jason:** I agree!

**WeiLing:** All I know is that I don't feel safe around here. They're so *mean*. Let's *do* something about it, you guys.

**Shamice:** I'm with *you*. I hate what's going on in this school *and* in my neighborhood. *Even* in my family. *None* of this is okay with me.

**Maya:** I think if we talk to Mrs. Rosen and Mr. King right now, it might help *change* something around here. *(Maya raises her hand and asks Mrs. Rosen and Mr. King to come over to talk with them)* Mrs. Rosen and Mr. King, we need to share something with you.

**Mrs. Rosen:** What is it, kids? Everyone looks so upset. What's wrong?

**Mr. King:** Is something going on that we can help you with?

**Shamice:** *(looks upset)* Yes, *a lot* is happening …

**Jason:** First, we heard Chuck and Daphne and all their friends insult WeiLing.

**Johnny:** They didn't let her sit with them for lunch.

**Mohammed:** And they said *really* mean things to her.

**Rosa:** They made her feel just *awful*.

**WeiLing:** It's true. I felt *so* hurt. I *still* do.

**David:** It was a bad scene, and when we spoke up to them, they were mean to *us*, too.

**Amani:** They threatened us.

**Jason:** And when I tried to tell them to cut it out, they bullied us even *more*, and I know when they get home, they're going to *cyberbully* us, too. *(Jason feels frustrated)* We go through this every single day, and we just don't know what to *do* about it.

**Maya:** Jason's right. We don't know what to do. Oh, and something else happened. We couldn't believe our eyes, but Georgie, Luther, Chuck, Gloria and Daphne suddenly started fighting with each *other*, too!

**WeiLing:** They were *so* mean! Bullying and pushing …

**Mr. King:** Wow. You're right. This *isn't* good, and thanks for sharing and trusting us. I can see why this kind of environment doesn't feel safe or comfortable for you. I had no *idea* all this was going on. We'll have a talk with them right now.

**Mrs. Rosen:** I agree. We've got to make constructive changes around here once and for all. Before we go over there, I'm inspired to compliment you. Some grownups aren't as aware as you are about the hurt that negative words and actions create. (*Mr. King nods his head in agreement*) You *already* understand this concept, and that gives me a lot of hope for our world. (*smiles*) Thanks, kids. Now enjoy the rest of your lunch in peace.

**Mr. King:** I agree, Mrs. Rosen. You *are* amazing, and I'm so glad you told us about this. Don't worry. We'll find a way to get through to them. Don't give up, okay?

**Maya:** (*smiles with relief*) Okay, we won't. Thanks for helping us. (*everyone agrees*)

**Mrs. Rosen:** That's what we're *here* for. Enjoy the pizza everybody!

(*Mrs. Rosen and Mr. King walk over to Georgie and his friends*)

**Mrs. Rosen:** Hi, everyone. How are you all doing today?

**Gloria:** We're good.

**Daphne:** Lunch is good, too. (*rolls eyes*) *For a change.*

**Mr. King:** I know what you mean. Sometimes it is and sometimes it isn't, but personally I think pizza is *always* good.

**Georgie:** Yeah, but I like *pepperoni* much more than plain.

**Luther:** Me too, Georgie! I like that more than any food in the whole world!

**Mrs. Rosen:** I tend to agree with you both. Pepperoni is *my* favorite, too. So, on a different subject … let's talk a little. You probably noticed that we were speaking with some of your classmates over there. They're feeling *very* upset about how they're being treated by you. Can you tell us more about that?

**Georgie:** We didn't do *anything*. They're just making it all up because they're against us.

**Daphne:** Ya, they're just babies complaining like that.

**Mr. King:** So, are you saying that *nothing* they said was true? You know, if what they told us *wasn't* true, that wouldn't be right of them to make it up … but if your behavior made them upset and the story *is* true, the *best* thing to do is to *admit* it, and then change the way you treat them right away.

**Mrs. Rosen:** Yes, and who knows, if you give them a chance, you might wind up with *new* friends!

**Gloria:** Well, to be honest, I guess we *weren't* so nice to WeiLing. We just didn't want anyone else to sit at our table. We needed privacy.

**Georgie:** That's true, Gloria, but we *were* kinda mean to her, and we told her that she wasn't *normal*.

**Luther:** And we said that she needed to go to another table. She wasn't welcome at ours.

**Chuck:** I guess we should have told her that we wanted to have our own space, and that maybe she could sit with us tomorrow.

**Mr. King:** Yes, that would have been a *much* better way to talk with her, Chuck. Good for you for realizing that, and thanks for admitting everything, too. You see, leaving someone out always hurts deep inside. I don't know if anyone has ever done that to *you*, but if it *has* happened, you *know* how it feels.

**Mrs. Rosen:** I know when that happens to me, I feel very sad, rejected and *deeply* hurt. People can be so cruel and insensitive, sometimes.

**Mr. King:** (*agrees*) They sure can, Mrs. Rosen. Kids, there's still another layer that we need to discuss. We were also told that when Jason and his friends spoke up for WeiLing, you bullied and threatened *them*, too. Is *that* true?

**Daphne:** (*hesitantly*) Um … ya. I'm afraid so. To be *really* honest with you, we even cyberbully them and say mean things online.

**Gloria:** We've gotten way out of control. We even started to be mean to each *other*, too.

**Luther:** Pushing each other and stuff.

**Mr. King:** You know, as hard as these issues are, your *honesty* is refreshing. Knowing *what* you did and how it makes a person feel is the first step towards changing for the better.

**Mrs. Rosen:** (*frowns and shows her disappointment*) That's true, Mr. King, but you know … this situation *does* surprise me a little. We have talked *a lot* about the negative effects of bullying in this school. (*sighs*) I guess there is still more work to do.

**Mr. King:** Think about this, kids. How would *you* feel if *you* were excluded? Threatened? Bullied? I think we need to use what happened here as a teaching and learning moment and offer you a *different* kind of homework today. We're going to give you an extra assignment that may help you understand the true meaning of friendship, respect for each other's feelings, and kindness.

---

**A Note to the Director:** Please feel free to choose a different book than the one listed below, and feel free to choose a different song, too.

---

**Mrs. Rosen:** To make sure you understand this concept, we are going to have you read a book called, *Secret of the Peaceful Warrior: A Story about Courage and Love,* by Dan

Millman. We would also like you to study the words to a song called, *"Imagine,"* by John Lennon and Yoko Ono. We want you to truly understand what the book and the song are saying to you personally.

**Mr. King:** And then after you read *"Peaceful Warrior"* and *"Imagine,"* we would like you to write an essay about what you have learned, and about the different choices *you* will make with each of your actions, words, feelings and thoughts.

**Mrs. Rosen:** How can your classmates feel good about being with you?

**Mr. King:** You know, kids … we can make a positive difference in each other's lives, and *everyone* has a special contribution to offer the world. *Including you.* And another thing … do you know that we want the same things in life, and it has *nothing* to do with money? We all want love, and we all want to be happy. We all want to have friends, and we all want to be accepted and included.

**Mrs. Rosen:** That's right. No matter where we're from, what we look like, what we believe, how much money we have or don't have … everyone breathes, cries, smiles and bleeds in the same way. We all share the same range of feelings, and our hearts all beat in the same way. Just think about how we are more alike than different …

**Mr. King:** We need to respect each other, and not become accusatory, mean and judgmental. *No one* is better than anyone else. We are all one community of love. At least … that's the goal. Like the song says, we are all "One Planet." Think about what we have discussed today, and how your words and the way you treated WeiLing must have made her feel.

**Mrs. Rosen:** And how your words and actions made Jason and his friends feel.

**Mr. King:** And the way you treated each other - how did that make you feel? Do you think you can work on changing your words and actions in our school, in your neighborhoods and in your homes? *I bet you can!* I *know* you have it in you to change! We will also call your parents and enlist *their* help with our *"Peace Begins with You and Me"* project.

**Mrs. Rosen:** How about changing right now by apologizing to WeiLing? Would you be willing to do that?

**Gloria:** (*nods*) Okay.

**Luther:** I really *do* feel bad about everything. Guess I didn't realize that everybody has feelings. (*reconsiders*) Actually … strike that. I *did* know. I just didn't care.

**Gloria:** I didn't care either, Luther. I do *now*. WeiLing didn't do anything to us, and we were so mean to her.

**Chuck:** I *want* to apologize!

**Daphne:** Me, too.

**Georgie:** Let's go ...

*(they walk up to WeiLing)*

**Chuck:** Hey, WeiLing. We're sorry about the way we treated you before. It wasn't *right*. *We* wouldn't like to be treated that way. Will you sit with us tomorrow and give us another chance?

**WeiLing:** Thanks for apologizing, you guys. I appreciate it. It does make me feel a little better.

**Gloria:** We really hope you'll give us another chance, okay?

**WeiLing:** Okay.

*(they walk over to Mr. King and Mrs. Rosen)*

**Daphne:** We apologized to WeiLing, and we really *are* sorry.

**Mrs. Rosen:** Thanks, kids. I'm so proud of you. That was a brave, courageous and honest action step. You've admitted everything, and you're taking responsibility and positive actions to change your behavior. Good for you!

**Mr. King:** I'm proud of you, too. Go ahead and finish up your lunch, and we'll see you in class for your "Life Lessons 101" assignment in about ten minutes. *(he turns to Jason and his friends)* Thanks for coming to us, kids.

**Jason:** *(smiles)* Thanks for listening and helping us out!

**Mrs. Rosen:** You were brave to share your problems with us. And by the way, don't worry if any kids in the school come up to you and say that you were tattling and telling on them. They need our "Life Lessons 101" assignment, too ... and we'll make *sure* they get it. What you did today is *more* than okay to do. Some things are just too *important* to keep to yourself, and adults can really help you out.

**Mr. King:** By speaking up, I think you helped create a change that could be very good for *everyone* around here.

> **Song Suggestions**: "The No Bully Rap – Song," from the album, "Celebrate" is a powerful and catchy rap, and the children love it. If the children are very young, or you would like to add a bit of humor, gentle movement and energy to the play at this juncture, you could also download a simple song called "Piece or Peace - A Seriously Silly Spelling Lesson." This song is also on "Celebrate." It involves the teachers, audience and students. As each letter is sung, the teachers, audience and children draw each letter in the air with their hands, hips, elbows and noses … and each time the chorus comes around, the song gets faster. Don't worry … the song slows down at the end, and the messages in each verse are powerful.

**Curtain Closes**

Act 1, Scene 3

## Kids Can Make a World of Difference

**Scene:** Outside.


**Narrator 1:** To make a long story short, the children, teachers and parents soon discovered new ways to teach the meaning of "*Peace Begins with You and Me.*" They also became more aware of the importance of their *own* role modeling, too.

**Narrator 2:** And as everyone in the school got to know each other better, they began to see that they had a great deal in *common*.

**Narrator 1:** Lots of the same feelings, thoughts, dreams, hopes, wishes and fears …

**Narrator 2:** And even though some kids still felt uncomfortable at school, most of them liked to hang around, act silly, and just have a really good time.

**Narrator 1:** But one day, despite how silly they liked to be with each other, they changed their mood and got into a very *serious* conversation.

**Narrator 2:** Let's listen in on Rosa and her friends right now ...


**Rosa:** You know, Maya, even though things *are* better around here, I don't understand why they are *still* trying to pick fights with me, even *after* their "Life Lessons 101" assignment.

**Maya:** I guess people don't change right away, Rosa. They need to be reminded every now and then.

**Rosa:** Yeah, that's true. I need reminders, too. But how they treat me gets me so angry! They don't even *know* me, Maya. They just judge me on the outside, and they don't take time to find out that I'm a really *great* person!

**Maya:** Rosa, I know it's tough. I don't know if this will make you feel any better, but you have *me* for a friend, you know. *(they give each other a hug)*

**Rosa:** I know, Maya. Our friendship means so much to me, too. It's just that *a lot* of things are bothering me right now …

**Maya:** What else?

**Rosa:** Well, I'm not getting along with my mother, the kids in my neighborhood are fighting with each other *all* the time, and then all the *gun shootings* and *violence* I hear about gets me scared. *(some of the other kids overhear the conversation and move towards them)*. It makes me feel so unsafe!

**Maya:** I can't stand that, either. Sometimes at night ... I have nightmares about it, Rosa. *(Amani overhears them and comes over with his friends)*

**Amani:** I just heard what you were saying, and I have a lot of the same feelings, too. But listen, you guys. Don't get so down. There are still more *good* people than bad people in our world. *Lots* more.

**Jason:** Amani is right. People help people every day. Lots of people don't care what color or religion you are, if you're rich or poor, or if you have a handicap.

**Mohammed:** That's true, Jason. And there are lots of people who *aren't* on drugs and *don't* believe in violence. They are kind and caring, and they help people wherever they go.

**Shamice:** You're right. We just hear all the *bad* stuff on TV and on social media. The good stuff doesn't get publicized as much for some reason.

**WeiLing:** That's true, and what you're saying gives me a lot of hope. I've *always* believed in what Anne Frank wrote in her diary during the holocaust. Even though she was going through a living nightmare, she said, "*I still believe, in spite of everything, people are truly good at heart.*"

**David:** Yeah, she was amazing. So *brave*, too. I also like that Gandhi said, "*An eye for an eye only makes the whole world blind.*" He was a great believer in peace and was saying that *no one* wins when there is violence. There are good and bad people everywhere, you guys. If *we* show that *we* care, *that's* the main thing. We need to do *our* part.

**Johnny:** You're right, David. It *starts* with us. I just wish *everyone* knew that. I don't like how people clump each other into one stereotype just because you look a certain way, or you believe in a certain religion, or you're just different from other people.

**Shamice:** I know. Unfair labels and name-calling happen to me all the time, Johnny. People think I can do things or not do things just because of how they judge me on the *outside*. It makes no *sense* to think like that!

**Rosa:** Wouldn't it be great if people just accepted each other for who they are, families got along better, kids stopped bullying, and if violence wasn't *anyone's* choice?

**Maya:** It sure *would* be great, Rosa. Most of all, just like Johnny said, I know that peace begins with me by how I choose to act *and* react.

**Amani:** You're right, Maya. If you really wanna know ... the way I see it ... it's not good when people don't respect each other. I think if someone is nice, it *helps* our world. If people are mean, it drags our *whole world* down! Least that's the way *I* see it ... and I'm usually right, you know. *(he laughs)*

**Kids:** Ya, you're perfect, Amani. *(they all laugh)*

**Jason:** But you *are* right, Amani. How we treat each other really *does* matter. The choices *we* make can create a vibration that the *whole world* feels! We just need to remember four things. I just think to myself … (*says each letter slowly*) **W-A-F-T**.

**Shamice:** (*scratches her head and frowns*) W-A-F-T? What's *that*, Jason?

**Jason:** (*chants it in a rhythmic rap and dramatizes*) Words, actions, feelings, thoughts … four special gifts that *can't* be bought.

**Shamice:** I get it! (*chants in a rhythmic rap*) The words we choose to say can feel good or bad … they can make someone smile, or make them feel sad …

**WeiLing:** (*chants in a rhythmic rap*) Words can be loving, or tear you apart …

**Maya:** (*chants in a rhythmic rap*) So, make sure you are talking from a loving *thinking* heart!

**Johnny:** (*coming out of his shell more*) That's awesome! I'm going to remember W-A-F-T, Jason! Thanks! You know … I thought of something to add that *nobody* mentioned.

**Rosa:** What, Johnny? Tell us.

**Johnny:** Well, part of making the world better is caring for our earth. The other day, my teacher told us something *great*. He said that Native Americans respect nature *so* much, they call the earth, "Mother Earth," and they call the sky, "Father Sky."

**Mohammed:** I like that too, Johnny. When the teacher was talking about it, I was sitting there wishing that *everybody* cared for the earth as much as that.

**David:** If we don't care about our earth, then *none* of us - no matter *what* we believe or don't believe - *none* of us will have a beautiful earth to even *live* on.

**WeiLing:** That's for *sure*, David.

**Shamice:** Good point! Hey, let's do the "Earth Rap!" Wanna? (*kids agree*)

## *Earth Rap*

## by Cheryl Melody

**Earth Chorus:** Save the earth, save the earth, come on now, save the earth!

**Shamice:** Well, I'm here to say we gotta keep the earth clean,
So the sky will stay blue, and the grass will stay green.

**Earth Chorus**

**Johnny:** Ride bikes. Walk more. Do it just like me!
Air smells good, air is clean, fresh as it can be!

**Earth Chorus**

**WeiLing, Rosa, Maya:** Recycle bottles, papers and cans,
Pick up the litter! *(they hold their noses)* Man, oh man!

**Earth Chorus**

**David, Amani, Mohammed and Jason:** Water? Lights? They're not free.
What else to say? Use them sparingly!

**Earth Chorus**

**Shamice:** People and animals need kindness and caring,

**All:** There's just *one* world we're loving and sharing!

**Earth Chorus**


**Rosa:** That was so much fun! You know, I feel a little better after talking with all of you. You're right about our earth, Johnny. We need to save the planet in so *many* ways.

**WeiLing:** Like driving cars *less* and walking *more*.

**Amani:** And reducing plastic, conserving water, and not leaving lights on.

**Rosa:** And loving and respecting nature, planting trees, and caring for all animals.

**Johnny:** There's so *much* that we can do to save the earth … *and* so much we can do to respect each other, too!

**Jason:** This *can* happen. People *can* change. *We* never used to get along, and now look!

**David:** Changes can happen *everywhere*.

**Shamice:** *(skeptical)* I don't know. This is a bit much. Let's get *real*, you guys! All the fighting and judging people ... that's just how things *are*! Like my parents say, "That's life!" There's *always* gonna be people who don't give themselves a chance to see what I'm *really* like, and maybe there's always gonna be violence, too.

**Maya:** *(discouraged)* You're right, Shamice. How are *we* gonna change all that - we're just *kids*!

**Mohammed:** *(sad and feeling helpless)* I agree. In my country, children are brought up with fighting, guns and war. There's *nothing* they can do about it. It's part of life there.

**David:** *(discouraged)* Mohammed, I know what you mean. The country where *my* parents grew up has been at war forever, too.

**Mohammed:** You know, David, I just wish people realized that even *if* they're different from each other, they can *still* be curious about the other person's way of life, and just get along.

**David:** *(brightens)* You're *right*, Mohammed. Look at *us*! *We* weren't sure that *we* would like each other at first, but then we started talking and realized that we were a lot more alike than we thought!

**Mohammed:** And now, we're great friends! Think about *that*, everybody. *This could happen all over the world*! I *know* it could!

*(enter Georgie, Luther, Daphne, Gloria and Chuck)*

**Jason:** Oh, boy. Here's comes trouble. Wonder if they'll be friendly today ...

**David:** Never mind them, Jason. I think they're really starting to get the message.

**Mohammed:** You're right, David. You aren't going to believe this, but some of them are coming over to my house today. Hey, everybody. Wanna come over, too? *(everyone is excited about the idea)*

**David:** You bet we would, Mohammed. We'll ask our parents and take it from there. I bet a lot of us will be able to come.

**Mohammed:** That would be *great*! I don't know if we'll wind up being friends with them, but we should give it a good try.

**Georgie:** *(waves to everybody)* Hey, you guys. See you later, Mohammed!

**Mohammed:** *(smiles)* Yeah, I can't wait. See you all later.

**All:** *(everyone is pleased with the positive changes at school, and they give each other an enthusiastic high-five)* **We did it!**

> **Song Suggestion:** "You Can Change You" from "Celebrate." Please note: If you are working with younger children or have a time restriction, the first act could be used for the entire play's message. If you do choose to end the play with Act One, I suggest that you end the play with the song, "One Planet," instead of "You Can Change You."

**Curtain Closes**

## Act 2, Scene 1

## Peace is a Verb

**Scene:** Outside. The kids are engaged in various activities. They are also listening to the narrators, too.

**Narrator 1:** You could just feel the positive changes in the air! For one thing, Georgie and his friends began to treat everyone with more respect, kindness and caring.

**Narrator 2:** Their negative attitude gradually disappeared, and soon they learned that they had more in common than they realized.

**Narrator 1:** *(turns to the nine kids)* Are we right, kids? *Has* the bullying cut down?

**Mohammed** *(walks over to them)* Yes, it's *much* better now. I don't feel as nervous around them anymore. *(turns to his friends)* Hey, you guys. I'm going to say it again! Maybe we could get the *whole world* to change like this!

**WeiLing:** *(shakes head and frowns)* I'm *still* not so sure about that one, Mohammed.

**David:** After all, how can *we* stop all the bullying? *We* don't have control over anyone's choices.

**Shamice:** You're right, David. We don't. And another thing … *(looks sad)* How can we stop all the abuse that some kids deal with at home and in other places, too?

**Rosa:** Yeah, that's true, Shamice. And what can *we* do about the drug problem? I mean the drug crisis is *real*. It's everywhere you look! *(she looks down and feels sad)* Even in my house.

**Johnny:** And one more thing? The fact that kids need to be on alert for someone who might come into their school with a gun and kill them … that's the *worst*! How can *we* solve this? *We're just kids.*

**Amani:** You're right, Johnny. These huge problems are bigger than any one of us can really manage!

**Maya:** And it's not just kids who are dealing with bullying, violence, drugs and abuse. It's happening to a lot of adults, too. Some of our own parents are putting up with all kinds of serious issues.

**Jason:** That's true, Maya. The worst thing is that a lot of us don't tell *anyone* about our problems.

**Mohammed**: I know. We just keep our suffering to ourselves. It's so sad.

**Amani:** It really *is* sad. We've got to share what's going on, and then we won't feel so alone.

**WeiLing:** And when we see someone threatened and we don't stand up for them … that's called *second-hand bullying*. When we're silent and don't help that person out, they feel all alone. It's the *same* as bullying them *ourselves!*

**Rosa:** (looks sad) Yeah, *I've* had times when no one stuck up for me … even though they witnessed the *whole* thing.

**Maya:** Sorry that's happened to you, Rosa. I'm afraid to admit that I've done a lot of second-hand bullying myself. I felt too *scared* to say anything. It takes courage to stick up for someone.

**David:** You're right, Maya. It *does* take courage. And since we're being so honest with each other, I need to tell you something *I've* done. In my other school, I used to bully kids … laugh right at them … exclude them … call them mean names … cyberbully … just so I could fit in with the tougher kids. I was afraid they would turn on *me* if I didn't act like that. *Inside* myself, I *knew* what I was doing was wrong. After all, *I* wouldn't want to be treated that way … and *that's* why I've changed.

> **A Note to the Director:** In the following dialogue, the subject of suicide is discussed, but if the subject feels inappropriate for the population of children that you are teaching, delete the dialogue *after* Shamice's lines. (*delete Amani, David and WeiLing's dialogue, and begin with Rosa's communication*)

**Shamice:** I'm glad you decided to change, David. (*looks sad*) Bullying causes deep wounds that you can't see sometimes, but it's *there*. Like you said before, Mohammed, the *saddest* thing is that we don't tell anyone how *much* we are suffering deep inside. We keep it a secret. I think that's why kids get depressed and feel so alone in the world.

**Amani:** (*looks upset*) Shamice, I bet that's why some kids commit suicide, too. They don't feel that there is anyone in the whole world they can confide in, and they just give up.

**Maya:** *We* should *never* give up, *no matter what*. We gotta always believe that things *will* change for the better. All I know is that you *gotta* keep hope and reach out for help when you need it!

**Weiling:** There are a lot of adults who would *want* to help us if they knew what we were going through. We should always reach out and talk to someone about our problems. Things might feel impossible right now, but there is *always* a solution.

**Rosa:** You're right about everything, you guys. And David, I'm so glad you changed how you used to act in the other school.

**David:** I'm glad I did too, Rosa.

**Rosa:** Hey, Johnny, what do you think about all this? You're kinda quiet.

**Johnny:** I don't know. I think what you're saying makes a lot of sense, but it's all too *big* to deal with. Who's going to listen to *us* about all the things we talked about? Bullying, drugs, violence, abuse, suicide … it's all just too much!

**WeiLing:** But Johnny, I know what we're talking about is big, but we gotta start *somewhere*! Like even if *we* find better ways to work out *our* disagreements, we'd be … what are the words my Mom used the other day?

**Maya:** Role models?

**WeiLIng:** Yeah, *that's* it! We'd be role models for the other kids, and then little by little maybe things *would* change …

**David:** I get it. You're saying how we treat ourselves and each other is the *real* meaning of "*Peace Begins with You and Me*." *We* are the mirrors of the kindness, love and respect that we want in our world. Just think about *that* everybody. Think about it!

> **Suggested Song:** "Peace is a Verb" from the album, "Celebrate"

**Maya:** Maybe hope *is* up to the kids, and every small change we make *does* matter.

**Shamice:** Think about this too, you guys. We are all *innocent* when we're born. Somehow along the way we *learn* prejudice and we learn not to like someone simply because they are different from us.

**Mohammed:** You're right. Prejudice *is* learned, but it doesn't *have* to be this way. I bet we could convince a lot of people to join our new "*Peace Begins with You and Me*" campaign!

**Amani:** You know what? I like this idea more and more. We can even ask for involvement from our parents, teachers, and other grownups. *A lot* of them feel like we do! They don't want violence either. I often hear my parents say that they're sick and tired of listening to all the *bad* news on the radio and on TV. They just want a loving world!

**Jason:** (*teases Amani good-naturedly*) You're right again, Amani.

**David:** And another thing. Sometimes I hear my mom and dad talking about how lucky we are to live in a country where we're free to share our opinions - a country with so *many* freedoms. They say that people are too indifferent and should get more involved.

**Shamice:** That's *sounds* good, but who's gonna listen to *us*? Usually people say to me, "*You've got a lot to learn about life, my dear girl.*"

**Johnny:** Or they say, *"Grow up, kid. You're dreaming. One person can't make a difference. The world is too messed up."*

**Rosa:** And here's another one I hear all the time … *"I think you've got your head in the clouds just dreaming things that can't happen. Get down to earth, girl."*

**Amani:** But we don't have to listen to those words! I can see that we're not just *any* kids. We're kids that really *care*!

**Jason:** Yup, you're right, Amani. My teacher says that each of us can make a difference in our world. I think we're onto something. If we can get people excited about our *"Peace Begins with You and Me"* campaign, who *knows* what could happen!

**WeiLing:** I'm with *you*! If we tell everyone about our idea… if we each make a Peace Promise … good things *will* start happening!

**Maya:** We can sprinkle magic seeds of peace all over the world! People will feel it and start to live like that, too! I'm *sure* of it. We just gotta work together!

**Jason:** Hey, just cause we're kids, *that* shouldn't matter! I bet there's stuff that we *all* can do … like try to get along with our families better …

**Mohammed:** And work out our problems with the kids around here …

**Shamice:** And put into practice the saying that my Grandpa says … *"Don't judge a book by its cover!"*

**Johnny:** And don't forget. We gotta protect Mother Earth and Father Sky!

**All:** *(they remember the "Earth Rap" and chant the chorus)* "Save the earth! Save the earth! Come on now! Save the earth!"

**Johnny:** Maybe our ideas *will* spread all over the world.

**Rosa:** I think that would be *great*. Thing is … I *still* don't know if it's possible.

**Johnny:** I know how we're gonna do it! We'll talk this over with other kids, the teachers, our parents, and other adults. Then, we'll announce this idea on the media. We'll tell *everyone* about our new *"Peace Begins with You and Me"* campaign.

**Rosa:** *(feels more hope)* You're right, Johnny. We can write letters to the United Nations and to every person who believes in the meaning of "being peace."

**Maya:** And maybe we can find a way to communicate with kids all around the world who care about these messages, too.

**Jason:** This is it! Maybe adults will pay attention to our messages even more *because* we're kids! *(turns to narrators)* You've been listening to our story. What do *you* think? Will people listen to us?

**Narrator 1:** I *know* they will, Jason!

**Narrator 2:** You are all truly amazing!

**WeiLing:** Let's go talk to the teachers about our idea!

**Rosa:** And after school, let's have a talk with our parents!

**Jason:** We'll talk with everyone and anyone who will listen to our "*Peace Begins with You and Me*" campaign!

**Shamice:** Let's get *everyone* to make one Peace Promise, and let's make our own promises, too.

**Johnny:** Yeah, let's *do* this, you guys! I'm so excited about this project, I'm bursting!

**Maya:** Me, too!

---

**Song Suggestion:** "Kids Can Make a World of Difference" (aka "One Day in Peace") from "Celebrate"

---

**Curtain Closes**

## Act 2, Scene 2

## Peace Promises

**Scene:** Weekend meeting at school that includes parents, teachers and children. As the children and adults plan ways to implement the *"Peace Begins with You and Me"* campaign, the air is electric with excitement.

**Narrator 1:** Look at this! Everyone is busy writing down Peace Promises.

**Narrator 2:** *(approaches a parent)* Excuse me for interrupting, Mrs. Kelly, but we were wondering if you could share the Peace Promise you just wrote …

**Mrs. Kelly:** Sure, I'd be happy to. I'm going to try to honor this one, too. *(Stands and turns to audience)* "As a parent, I promise to count to 20 before losing my cool with my kids. I'm also going to listen to their feelings more. I mean … *really* listen." (*audience, parents, teachers and children applaud and make positive comments*)

**Mr. Campbell:** (Parent) That's *impressive*, Mrs. Kelly.

**Mrs. Kelly:** (Parent) (*said in the spirit of fun*) Why, *thank you*, Mr. Campbell.

**Mr. Campbell:** Seriously, I'm going to aim for that, too. (*turns to audience*) Mine says, "I will be more patient as a husband, father, at work, when I drive, when I shop … in everything I do. Life isn't all about me. I'm going to be more open-hearted and kind to the people I know, and even to the strangers that I meet. It doesn't cost anything to smile at a stranger, and who knows, it might brighten their day! *Everyone* deserves respect and kindness." (*audience, parents, teachers and children applaud and make positive comments*)

**Eva:** (raises hand) I've got a whole *bunch* of promises, too! Ready, everybody?

**Mrs. Rosen:** (*smiles warmly*) We're ready, Eva. Thanks for your enthusiasm!

**Eva:** (*confident and proud*) No problem, Mrs. Rosen. I *like* this assignment! "I promise to be a good example to others, listen to people I disagree with, *never* use violence, be kind to my parents, and *even* be nicer to my sister over there. (*Maya and Eva smile and wave at each other, and everyone laughs warmly and applauds*)

**Daniel:** (*raises hand*) I made some promises, too!

**Mr. King:** Well, let's hear them, Daniel.

**Daniel:** "I promise to think *before* I speak, and I also promise not to bully or call people names. (*audience, parents, teachers and children applaud and make positive comments*)

**Mr. Jackson:** (Parent) Wow! Those are really great promises, Daniel. Makes me feel better about everything!

**Daniel:** Thanks, Mr. Jackson. I *mean* them, too. (*Mr. Jackson gives him a thumbs up*)

**Emily:** And here's all of mine.

**Mrs. Patel:** I can't wait to hear them, Emily. It's such a breath of fresh air to hear all these wonderful promises. (*all the parents, teachers and children agree*)

**Emily:** Thanks, Mrs. Patel. Here goes … "I promise not to take drugs like my brother does, and I promise to take care of my body. I will always tell the truth, include all people, share what I have, be grateful, forgive others, and not fight." (*everyone applauds*)

**Mr. King:** These promises are wonderful!

**Jeremy:** *(raises hand)* I only have one promise, but it's powerful and it means a lot to me.

**Mr. Goldberg:** I'd love to hear it, Jeremy. You are inspiring me to make one, too.

**Jeremy:** Anytime I can be *your* role model, Mr. Goldberg. (*everyone laughs*) "I promise to help people who don't even have enough money to buy food or live in a safe place. I'm going to do everything I can to help people who aren't as lucky as me." (*everyone applauds*)

**Mr. Goldberg:** (Parent) (*smiles at Jeremy*) Well, I told you I would be inspired! "I promise to care for the earth by being more aware of conservation and preservation. I also promise to be fully present with the person that wants my attention. I will put my cell phone down, and just listen with an open heart and mind. (*Jeremy gives Mr. Goldberg a thumbs up, and* the *audience, parents, teachers and children applaud and make positive comments*)

---

**A Note to the Director:** Feel free to expand your cast with more children, emphasizing any new awareness that has been heightened in your school.

---

**Narrator 1:** (*speaks to audience*) There were so *many* Peace Promises made that day, and everyone felt hope for themselves, each other and the world.

**Narrator 2:** Kids and adults were changing for the better … families were getting along, kids were much more aware of what they said and did to each other, and the teachers were inspired to do whatever they could to support the vision for "*Peace Begins with You and Me*."

**Narrator 1:** Everyone made a commitment to help the children's dream for "*Peace Begins with You and Me*" come true.

**Mrs. Rosen, Teacher:** Our meeting has already been so exciting! Thank you for giving up a day on a weekend to support an amazing idea created by our children! Your Peace Promises are spectacular! Before we go any further in our implementation process, I wanted to make sure that everyone understands the true meaning of *"Peace Begins with You and Me."* Let's review a little. Anyone?

**Daphne:** It means to work our issues out without fighting and name-calling. Listen to the other person's point of view, and not judge other kids just because they seem different from me. (*everyone agrees and cheers*)

**Gloria:** I'm with you, Daphne. Not picking on other kids, gossiping behind someone's back, teasing them, bullying ... you know ... all the stuff we used to do. Everybody has the same feelings, and we *all* want to be accepted and loved. I *get* that now.

**Georgie:** I don't want to be a part of that scene any more.

**Luther and Chuck:** Me, either ...

**Shamice:** Another thing?

**Mrs. Rosen:** Yes, Shamice?

**Shamice:** I think *"Peace Begins with You and Me"* means that we shouldn't leave someone out just because they're different from us. We should include them, no matter what. (*everyone agrees*)

**Eva:** That's true, Shamice. And also? People shouldn't hurt animals. I love animals. They should have respect, too. (*everyone agrees*)

**Daniel:** And we should help people who aren't as lucky as us. There are a lot of people who go hungry. They don't have enough money for food ... or *even* a place to live.

**Emily:** We should give them some of *our* food. (*everyone agrees*)

**Mrs. Patel:** These kids are right! I haven't been doing enough!

**Mr. Jackson:** Me, either!

**WeiLing:** We need to realize that everybody isn't as lucky as us.

**David:** I guess there are people who have a *real* rough time of it. My family has money problems, but not as bad as some other people!

**Johnny:** I know what you mean, David. And I thought of something else, too. Part of peace is caring about ourselves and our bodies. You know ... not smoking, drinking, taking drugs. These things can *really* mess you up!

**Maya:** That's for sure, Johnny. *And* we need to remember the words to the song we learned the other day ... *Shake your **own** hand,* and always say ...

**ALL:** *I'm an amazing person today!*

> **Song Suggestions:** "Shake Your Own Hand, from the album, "Celebrate," or if the children are young, download "The Friendship Song" on 'Songs That Make the Heart Feel Good."

**Rosa:** *Shake your own hand.* I like those words. We shouldn't be so hard on ourselves when we mess up. It's *okay* to make mistakes. That's how we *learn*. Don't put yourself down, and if anybody *else* puts you down, brush it away. What they're saying is not true about you. *Believe in yourself*!

> **A Note to the Director:** The following rap is a verse from "The No Bully Rap - Song" from the album, "Celebrate."

**Gloria:** I know one thing … I'm changing for the better already. I'm not going to mess other people up by putting them down any more. It doesn't make me feel *good* to do that. Like the "*The No Bully Rap - Song*" says …

**Gloria*:*** *The nicer you are … to yourself …*

**Maya:** *The less you'll pick on somebody else.*

**Amani and Georgie:** *And nobody can take away your hopes or your dreams!*

**Shamice and Luther:** *Keep them alive as hard as it seems.*

**David and Chuck:** *You might have money, or you might be broke.*

**Johnny and Daphne:** *But we're all the same with a thing called HOPE.*

**Mohammed:** *Hopes are the dreams alive in your mind …*

**WeiLing:** *Discover all you can be!*

**Jason and Maya:** *That's a treasure only* **you** *have the* **power** *to find!*

**Mrs. Rosen:** I can tell that you've been thinking *a lot* this subject. You're right. How each of us behaves towards ourselves and each other affects the vibration of the whole world.

**Mr. King:** That's so true! I also see that your artwork on "being peace" is all over our school. They are fantastic expressions of what peace can be! How would you feel about also creating "*Peace Begins with You and Me*" essays? Could you write down what *this* kind of peace means to you personally?

**Mrs. Rosen:** If you prefer, you could write original "*Peace Begins with You and Me*" poems, songs … even raps.

**WeiLing:** I like *all* these ideas. I *love* expressing myself through writing, music and art!

**Rosa:** Me, too! And how about forming *"Peace Begins with You and Me"* Clubs? Could we do that, too?

**Mrs. Rosen:** Yes to everything! This is *wonderful*!

**Mr. King:** I'd love to help *form* your Peace Clubs!

**Mr. Casey:** (Teacher): This really *is* a terrific idea, Rosa. I know I'd like to help get that started, too.

**Rosa:** Wow, thanks. This is great!

**Mrs. Bourgette** (Teacher): And I know a lot about creating peace-themed websites. There are people all over the world who would respond to your *"Peace Begins with You and Me"* dream. I bet they would even post their own Peace Promises on your website.

**Mrs. Rosen:** And since I teach history, this would be a great chance to explore different cultures from all over the world. Let's put big maps in every classroom, and as soon as we hear from someone from another country, we could learn about the people there … their history, geography, different cultures, customs, beliefs … What do you say we get started right away?

**Kids:** Sounds good to us!

**Curtain Closes**

## Act 3, Scene 1

## An Important Letter is Sent

**Narrator 1:** The "*Peace Begins with You and Me*" campaign was filled with essays, art projects, original songs, poems, Peace Promises, raps and Peace Clubs, and the excitement in this school traveled to other schools, homes and neighborhoods. Everyone worked together.

**Narrator 2:** Websites for peace were created, and now people all over the world are responding!

**Narrator 1:** Do you see the magic in what just a few kids started? Remember how discouraged these children felt in the beginning of the story? Now, look at them! They've really taken charge!

**Narrator 2:** Do you see what can be possible if we all have a common vision? And the work isn't done yet. Everyday, kids, teachers and parents make sure that they follow through on every plan.

**Narrator 1:** Yes, people all over the world are responding by writing their own "*Peace Begins with You and Me*" songs, essays, raps and Peace Promises. They are even forming *International* Peace Clubs. It's amazing!

**Narrator 2:** What these children accomplished in such a short time shows that each of us can be an everyday hero for ourselves and each other! Let's listen to one of their letters, now ...

*(one child reads the letter, or the letter can be read as a group)*

### AN IMPORTANT LETTER IS SENT

To the People of the World and to The United Nations ...

We, the Children of the World, hereby announce that peace *can* happen. It begins with *each* of us ... with the words we choose to say, the thoughts we think, how we treat each other, and by respecting each person's feelings. We want *everyone* to realize that peace isn't about the world out there somewhere. It's about each one of us. Let's work together by listening to each other, and by working out our differences nonviolently. Please make your own Peace Promise and join our campaign today!

Signed,

The Children of the World

**Narrrator 1:** Peace Promises soon began to pour in!

**Narrator 2:** Suddenly their small circle of friends became bigger, forming links in a worldwide chain. It was almost like you could *"see"* peace spreading … as if there were little lights on a map of the world, and every time a new person created a *"Peace Begins with You and Me"* promise, a light would glow throughout the whole world.

**Narrator 1:** Everyone was filled with excitement and hope. They could just *feel* the magic in what they were doing together. It seemed as if people had been waiting for someone to do this, and the dream of creating a more peaceful and loving world was so close … the children could taste it.

> **Song Suggestion:** "Wishes" from the album, "Songs That Make the Heart Feel Good"

**Curtain Closes**

## Act 3, Scene 2

## The Children's Dream

**Scene:** Classroom. Georgie notices an official-looking letter on Mrs. Rosen's desk.

**Georgie:** Mrs. Rosen? Is that a new letter for us? It looks very important.

**Mrs. Rosen:** Yes, it is. It's an amazing letter, Georgie. Would you like to read it to everyone? *(the kids are buzzing with excitement)*

**WeiLIng:** Where is it from, Georgie?

**Amani:** Who wrote it?

**Georgie:** *(Georgie is very dramatic)* Wait a minute, wait a minute. Let *me* handle this … Wow! It's from people all over the world! *(clears his throat)*

### AN IMPORTANT LETTER IS RECEIVED

To the Children of the World …

Thank you for being the role models and leaders of your *"Peace Begins with You and Me"* campaign. Because of your letter, we promise to work even harder to be better people in what we choose to say, think, feel and do inside ourselves, in our homes, schools, workplaces and neighborhoods. Enclosed are just some of the *"Peace Begins with You and Me"* promises that were collected. *(he takes out a long scroll of paper filled with promises from people all over the world)*. We agree with your mission, and we will do our part to help your dream come true. You are right, kids. Each one of us *can* and *do* make a difference with the positive power of our words, thoughts, feelings and actions.

Signed,

The People of the World and The United Nations

**Luther:** WOW!

**Mohammed:** That's sooo cool!

**Mrs. Kelly:** Amazing!

**Chuck:** Look what *we* started!

**Shamice:** I can't believe it!

**Narrator 1:** (*talks with the audience*) What an important letter! The children were *sure* that word would get out even *more* now!

**Narrator 2:** (*asks audience*) You know … The response to this letter makes me wonder, audience … maybe *you* could think of a Peace Promise, too …

*(children address the audience, stepping forward one by one)*

**Shamice:** How can *you* add *your* voice? If we can offer respect and love to each other for just *one* day …

**Amani:** Then it will happen on *lots* of days.

**Johnny:** And you can create this positive vibration.

**Daphne:** Every idea and action step counts.

**Georgie:** *We* made Peace Promises. How about you? How could you change your own behavior? Could your words be more positive? Could you do more to help people feel loved and included? See yourself really *doing* what your Peace Promise says, and then … make it happen for real!

**Mohammed:** Be aware of your own W-A-F-T – words, actions, feelings and thoughts.

**WeiLing:** Keep our vision of "being peace" in your mind and heart. Don't *ever* give up.

**Rosa:** Always keep hope. You can have this dream, too!

**David:** Imagine a world where we respect each other's differences and are curious about learning more about other people's cultures.

**Gloria:** Imagine a world where we can solve differences nonviolently.

**Chuck:** A world where people talk things out instead of fighting.

**Luther:** They treat people the way *they* want to be treated. With equal respect and acceptance.

**Maya:** Let's light a candle in our homes to remind us how the world can shine when it celebrates the true meaning of "*Peace Begins with You and Me.*"

**Jason:** We need your support. Let's work together to help make a better world.

**Cast:** *Are you in, audience?*

---

**A Note to the Director:** Hold up a large poster with "**YES**" on it and have the cast encourage the audience to get involved by saying …

**Audience:** YES!

**Rosa:** Great! Together, we can make *amazing* changes.

**Georgie:** We can create a kinder and more caring world.

**WeiLing:** The sky has no limit, and there is no limit to what we can do together!

## *The Peace Begins with You and Me Pledge*

**All:** I know … that peace … begins … with you and with me …

**Solo:** Inside ourselves …

**Solo:** In our homes …

**Solo:** In our schools …

**Solo:** In every workplace …

**Solo:** In our neighbohoods …

**Solo:** And on Mother Earth …

**Solo:** Let's speak words that are kind.

**Solo:** Think thoughts that don't make fun or judge.

**Solo:** Include people that are different from us.

**Solo:** And respect each other's feelings.

**All:** *We* are the changes we wish for in the world.

**Solo:** Let's *be* there for each other.

**All:** Because peace begins with me and peace begins with you!

---

**Song Suggestion:** "One Planet." This song could be sung with the entire cast, and even with the audience. Add languages for "hello," "welcome" and "peace" at the beginning and at the end of the song. "One Planet" can be found on Amazon Music, Apple Music, CD Baby and iTunes, and on the albums, "Celebrate," "Friends Forever" and "World Peace – The Children's Dream." It can also be heard on www.cherylmelody.com

## "One Planet"

by Cheryl Melody

**Chorus**
We're all one people, (*spoken: "Hello" - English; "Jambo" - Swahili*)
All one nation, (*spoken: "Hola" - Spanish; "Salaam" - Arabic*)
All one planet, (*spoken: "Kon'ichiwa" - Japanese; "Ni hao" - Chinese*)
Together we can live. (*spoken: "Aloha" - Hawaiian; "Guten Tag" - German*)

**Chorus**
We're all one people,
All one nation,
All one planet,
Together we can live.

Verse 1:
We're all the colors of one rainbow,
All the feelings of one heart,
All the music of one voice,
Let's reach for a brand-new start.

**Chorus**

Verse 2:
Lots of struggles are the same for all of us,
Each other's hearts we really do know.
We're all connected with each other,
Remember that, and don't feel low.

**Chorus**

Verse 3:
Show your kindness to each other,
Know that we are one.
There's magic in caring for another,
Your love shines like the sun.

**Chorus**

Verse 4:
Sing this song to each other,
Dance with joy hand-in-hand.
We're everybody's sister and brother,
So, strike up the _____ (*add the name of your school*) "One Planet" band!

**Chorus**

We're all one people, (*spoken: "Adios" – Spanish*)
All one nation, (*spoken: "Shalom" – Hebrew – hello, goodbye and peace*)
All one planet, (*spoken: "Namaste" – Sanskrit/Hindu - Peace*)
Together we can live. (*spoken: "Heiwa" – Japanese - Peace*)


**All: We ... did it!** *(high-five, hugs and smiles)*


**Curtain Closes**

# "Shift of Heart"

by Cheryl Melody Baskin

Dear Amazing One,

Thank you for working so hard with the children and choosing to perform *"Peace Begins with You and Me."* To continue to inspire you to keep hope in your own heart, I have enclosed an extra gift that is just for you. It is an original poem called "Shift of Heart." Thank you again for believing that it is possible to have a world of unconditional love, peace and hope, one by one by one by one.

Dear Peace Seekers,

Envision with me a Shift of Heart in all people who seek revenge.
A Shift of Heart on each side …
In those who hate,
And in those who are hated.

Imagine with me a day when those who have the power to destroy the world …
Feel a transformational shift in their heart to save the world.

Search with me for all people to understand one another,
And if we can't understand one another …
May we at least, at the very least
Respect one another's differences.

Hope with me that each one of us finds
Inner peace, inner love, inner compassion and inner forgiveness …
And because of these qualities felt from within,
There will and can be a Shift of Heart towards each other.

Visualize with me sending a glorious beaming light
Through and around ourselves, each other and Mother Earth.
Let every living being suddenly feel love, transformation,
Celebration, tolerance and peace.

And may there be a Shift of Heart within all people of our small precious world.

## About the Author ...

**Cheryl Melody Baskin** is a "you can change your life" author, playwright, healing arts and creativity specialist, motivational speaker, educator, intuitive life coach, workshop facilitator, performing artist, award-winning recording artist and sound healer. She has always been a starry-eyed dreamer of dreams and is a strong believer in listening to life's wisdom-whispers, trusting in the magical mystery of the unknown, healing from inside-out, holding a vision for peace, and walking the path of love. Her passion is to inspire anyone with a dream to take a leap of faith towards living it.

In addition to the children's play, *"Peace Begins with You and Me,"* Cheryl Melody Baskin is also the author of a bestselling motivational self-help book entitled *"Heart-Dreamer: Stepping into Life, Love, Creativity and Dreams - No Matter What."* Its purpose is to inspire readers to discover, honor and actualize their innermost truth, hopes and dreams. *"Heart-Dreamer"* overflows with encouragement, life wisdom, experiential self-discovery activities, healing tools for inner peace, creativity exercises and an abundance of unconditional love and support. It also contains the voices of wisdom from people all around the globe.

*New York Times* bestselling author and innovative physician, Dr. Bernie Siegel said, "As soon as I saw the sentence, "allow your heart to guide you," I knew Melody's words contained the truth about life." United Nations Humanitarian Artist, Conservationist and Grammy award winner, Ricky Kej said, "This brilliant and life-changing book causes us to do a bit of soul-searching to find answers to our innumerable inner questions. *Heart-Dreamer* is not just a book, it is a way of life."

*"Shift of Heart - Paths to Healing and Love"* is Cheryl Melody Baskin's first book, and as award-winning writer, Zorina Frey states, "It's like getting a big hug." Bestselling author, Tama Kieves says, "She urges us, at any age, to fall in love with our lives, even in chaos, and to experience inner healing and a shift of heart."

As a musician with the stage name of "Cheryl Melody," she has recorded six award-winning albums with positive messages for children and three albums with healing and positive messages for adults. The albums for adults include *"Listen to the Whispers," "Lullabies of Love"* and *"Voice of the Angels - A Healing Journey,"* along with a multigenerational album entitled, *"Celebrate."*

Her preferred first name is "Melody," and of all the songs that she has written, her favorite song is *"If You Have a Dream."* She is also the founder and moderator of a large Facebook community called "Shift of Heart."

# Contact Information

Digital downloads for all songs written by "Cheryl Melody" can be purchased on Amazon, Apple Music, CD Baby or iTunes.

## Albums:

- *Celebrate!* - Multigenerational
- *World Peace - The Children's Dream* - Children
- *Friends Forever* - Children
- *Songs That Make the Heart Feel Good* - Children
- *Let's Pretend and More!* - Children
- *Peek-a-boo, I Love You!* - Children
- *Lullabies of Love* - Adults
- *Listen to the Whispers* - Adults
- *Voice of the Angels - A Healing Journey* - Adults

## Paperbacks and eBooks

Titles by Cheryl Melody Baskin include the following motivational self-help books:

- *"Heart-Dreamer: Stepping into Life, Love, Creativity and Dreams - No Matter What"*

- *"Shift of Heart - Paths to Healing and Love"*

- *"Peace Begins with You and Me"*

Join my Facebook *Shift of Heart* Community!
https://www.facebook.com/groups/103850356767217/

Website: www.cherylmelody.com

Email: cherylmelody@gmail.com

## With a Grateful Heart

**Bob Silverstein:** Thank you for being the first seed that inspired me to create *"Peace Begins with You and Me"* and the album, *"World Peace - The Children's Dream."* You have made a difference in my life and in the lives of many children across the world. I am forever grateful that our lives, purpose and passion for peace connected during that serendipitous and amazing time period.

**Deborah Burke Henderson:** Thank you so much for reading drafts of the peace play, and for providing me with such wonderful edits, suggestions, encouragement and support … and for even providing ideas for its implementation into the world! I am so grateful. You are not only a great writer, reporter and gifted public relations expert, your open heart and generosity is a gift to all who know you … and especially a gift to me.

**Ann Marie Speicher:** Thank you for reading the manuscripts of both *"Heart-Dreamer"* and *"Peace Begins with You and Me,"* and for writing beautiful testimonials on behalf of both projects in the middle of a busy life. The best part about reaching out to you is that we have become friends … and thank you again for all your encouragement. Writing my books and plays at the library led me to a stellar librarian (you), and it's been a joy to have your support, big heart and light shine towards me.

**Veronica Yager:** Thank you for your professionalism, creativity and caring heart. https://yellowstudiosonline.com

**Teachers/Directors:** Thank you for choosing an educational values-based play. You had many other choices, and it speaks volumes about your own values and who you are as a person to have decided on *"Peace Begins with You and Me"* over so many other school musicals. This choice took a special kind of courage and a special kind of person, and I am grateful that we have connected in this way. Thank you for all you are and do to shine more love into the world.

**To all the Peacemakers on our precious planet:** Thank you for working with me to keep a vision for peace, hope and love alive - no matter what. The only behaviors that we can control are our own … by being mindful of the quality of our words, actions, thoughts and feelings. As the children in the play say, "It's not about the world out there. It's about each one of us." I am comforted and grateful that you travel the *"Peace Begins with You and Me"* path and serve as role models for a better world along with me. We are all human and make mistakes, but as long as we are try to grow from inside-out, forgive, embrace compassion, empathy and nonjudgment, we stimulate the vision and the possibility that peace will one day exist throughout the entire world. Thank you for paving the way towards a higher consciousness. Your courage, leadership, strength and unconditional love serve as a guiding light for all of us.

## *"Peace Begins with You and Me"*

## Song Lyrics

*Three Words* (The lyrics are enclosed in the script) | Page 4

*One Planet* | Page 52

*Friends Forever* | Page 53

*The No Bully Rap - Song* | Page 54

*P-i-e-c-e or P-e-a-c-e? A Seriously Silly Spelling Song* | Page 55

*W-A-F-T* (The lyrics are enclosed in the script) | Page 26

*Earth Rap* (The lyrics are enclosed in the script) | Page 27

*You Can Change You* | Page 56

*Peace is a Verb* | Page 57

*Kids Can Make a World of Difference* | Page 58

*Shake Your Own Hand* | Page 59

*Wishes* | Page 60

*If You Have a Dream* (Bonus Song) | Page 61

\*All songs are written and sung by Cheryl Melody. They can be found on Amazon Music, Apple Music, CD Baby and iTunes.

## *One Planet*

This song can be found on Amazon Music, Apple Music, CD Baby and iTunes. It is also part of the albums, "Celebrate" and "Friends Forever."

**Earth Chorus:** We're all one people, (*spoken: "Hello" - English; "Jambo" - Swahili*)
All one nation, (*spoken: "Hola" - Spanish; "Salaam" - Arabic*)
All one planet, (*spoken: "Kon'ichiwa" - Japanese; "Ni hao" - Chinese*)
Together we can live. (*spoken: "Aloha" - Hawaiian; "Guten Tag" - German*)

**Earth Chorus:** We're all one people,
All one global nation,
All one planet,
Together we can live.

Verse 1: We're all the colors of one rainbow,
All the feelings of one heart,
All the music of one voice,
Let's reach for a brand-new start. (**Earth Chorus**)

Verse 2: Lots of struggles are the same for all of us,
Each other's hearts we really do know.
We're all connected with each other,
Remember that, and don't feel low. (**Earth Chorus**)

Verse 3: Show your kindness to each other,
Know that we are one.
There's magic in caring for another,
Your love shines like the sun. (**Earth Chorus**)

Verse 4: Sing this song to each other,
Dance with joy hand-in-hand.
We're everybody's sister and brother,
So, strike up the _____ "One Planet" band! (*add the name of your school*)

**Earth Chorus**

We're all one people, (*spoken: "Adios" – Spanish*)
All one nation, (*spoken: "Shalom" – Hebrew – hello, goodbye and peace*)
All one planet, (*spoken: "Namaste" – Sanskrit/Hindu - Peace*)
Together we can live. (*spoken: "Heiwa" – Japanese - Peace*)

## *Friends Forever*

This song can be found on Amazon Music, Apple Music, CD Baby and iTunes. It is also part of the *"Friends Forever"* album.

**(Group 1)** I want to be your friend, every single day.
A friendship with no end, caring in every way.
Playing and talking and listening to you,
Sharing together, deciding what to do.
I want to be your friend, every single day.

**(Group 2)** I want to be your friend too, whenever you're happy or blue.
I'll be your friend indeed, whenever you want or need.
Playing and talking and listening to you,
Sharing together, deciding what to do.
I want to be your friend too, whenever you're happy or blue.

**Earth Chorus**
Good friends forever, good friends are we,
Good friends forever, friends we'll always be.
I want to be your friend,
Every single day.

**(Group 1)** "Friends forever?"
**(Group 2)** "Friends forever!"

## *The No Bully Rap – Song*

This song is on Amazon Music, Apple Music, CD Baby and iTunes. It is also part of the *"Celebrate"* album.

(*rap/spoken word*) Once upon a time there were some really great kids,
But they were made fun of no matter what they did.
There was Rosa, Shamice, Mohammed and David,
And the bullies over there called them names that they hated.
But these great kids, they knew just what to do,
They said, "Let's get together, we'll see this through,"
So, they walked right up, looked those kids in the eyes,
Said, "We have some ideas, so listen up, you guys!"

**Earth Chorus:** I've got feelings, you've got feelings, everyone's got 'em, too!
Let's find some ways to get along by what we say and do.
Respect yourself, respect each other, try to get along …
Come and join the *Peace Begins with You and Me* side,
It's the no bully, no teasing, no gossip song.

(*spoken word*) Here's some hints on how to work it, cool it, be it, treat each other good.
Dealing with each other in a manner we really should.

Being a bully or being a tease, don't be that way, please oh please.
Cause it makes for mad feelings, sad as can be,
Drags our whole world down, can't you see …
That a kid can only take so much of mean words or angry touch.
Some people might be different, they might not fit in,
But teasing them – that's a *no* win!

**Earth Chorus**

And the nicer you are to yourself, the less you'll pick on somebody else.
And nobody can take away your hopes or your dreams,
Keep them alive, as hard as it seems.
You might have money, or you might be broke,
But we're all the same with a thing called hope.
Hopes are the dreams alive in your mind,
Discover all you can *be* – it's a treasure only *you* have the *power* to find!

**Earth Chorus**

(*ending*) Skit Skat dittin dat, what do you think of that?
Dittin dattin dittin, it's the *No Bully Rap*!
Bully, gossip, tease? Not a cool way.
Let's watch what we do and think and say!

Oh, yeah! Skit Skat!

## *P-i-e-c-e or P-e-a-c-e? A Seriously Silly Spelling Lesson*

This song is on Amazon Music, Apple Music, CD Baby and iTunes. It is also part of the "*Celebrate*" album.

**A note to Director:** Choose five children to hold up each of the letters in the word, "P-E-A-C-E."

**Earth Chorus**: P-E-A-C-E, P-E-A-C-E

Verse 1: (*sung by a group of teachers*) It's not a piece of pie, not a piece of cake,
Not a piece of this or that, nothing that we bake.
That's ... *(elongate "that's")*
(*spoken word by teachers*) Ready? Begin! (**Earth Chorus**)

(*one teacher continues in spoken word*) Here is what this kind of peace is *not* ...
Did you ever want to fight and fight? Only say that *you* are right?
Tease someone? Even hit? Maybe throw a *giant fit*?!
(*sung by a teacher*) Well, my friends, that's not ...
(*spoken word*) Ready? Begin! (**Earth Chorus**)

(*Spoken word by teachers*) The words we choose to say can feel good or bad,
They can make someone smile or make them feel so sad.
(*sung by a teacher*) Words can be loving, or tear somebody apart,
So, make sure you are talking from a loving *thinking* heart.
That's ... (*elongate the note*) (**Earth Chorus**)

(*spoken word by a teacher*) Your hands can help, or your hands can fight,
Make sure you're using them in a way that's right.
(*sung by teachers*) Open your hands and open your heart,
Care about each other from the very start.
That's ... (*elongate "That's"*) (**Earth Chorus**)

(*sung by a teacher*) And remember to be good to you,
Don't hurt yourself by what you say to yourself or do.
(*spoken word*) Say, "I'm doing the best I can for who I am right now."
(*sung*) Because peace begins inside of us, then spreads around without much fuss. (**Earth Chorus**)

(*sung by teachers*) You spelled it right in every way, that's the kind of peace we say.
Peace inside, then peace on earth, everyday!
That's ... (*elongate "that's"*) ...

(**Earth Chorus**) P-E-A-C-E (*go faster and faster with each of the letters and body gestures, repeating four times, and then slowing it down*).

Spells ... Peace! (*end with one or more beautiful tones for the word, "Peace," sung by both children and adults*)

## *You Can Change You!*

This song is found on Amazon Music, Apple Music, CD Baby and iTunes. It is also part of the album, *"Celebrate."*

Today is the first day of the rest of your life,
And you can change you.
Don't judge a book by its cover.

Think before you act now …
Don't do it if it hurts someone else!

Think before you talk now …
Don't say it if it hurts someone else!

Think before you judge now …
Don't even think it if it hurts someone else!

Cause what you say and what you think and what you do …
Is a reflection in the mirror … of you!

Show the good, inside you,
Say the good, inside you,
Feel the good, inside you,
Spread the good, inside you,
Do the good, inside you,
I know there's good, inside you.

Today is the first day of the rest of your life,
And you can change you.
Don't judge a book by its cover.

Work it out, work your differences …
Work it out, work your differences …

You can change you!

## *Peace is a Verb*

This song can be found on Amazon Music, Apple Music, CD Baby and iTunes. It is also part of the album, *"Celebrate."*

**Earth Chorus**
Think about it, think about it, think about it …
What could you do?
Be a Peacemaker, listen for peace clues,
Make your own promises and follow them through.

Verse 1: Peace could be as simple as looking into somebody's eyes …
Somebody you never gave a chance to before,
A new friend can be a totally cool surprise.

**Earth Chorus**

Verse 2: I promise to say more thank you's,
I promise to say more please's,
I promise to say, "You're welcome,"
Or bless you if somebody sneezes … (*one child: "Ah ah … choo!"*) (*chorus: "Bless you!"*)

**Earth Chorus**

Verse 3: I promise to hold the door for somebody,
I won't push you around.
Instead of talking, talk, talk, talk,
I'll listen to your feelings without a sound (*"then I hope you'll listen to me too"*)

**Earth Chorus**

Verse 4: I promise to help Mrs. McFee,
Cause she is one of the elderly.
I'll use my words instead of fight,
And I won't say I'm the only one that's right!

**Earth Chorus**

Verse 5: Help make a world of peace,
A world of joy and caring.
Help make a bully free world,
It's your ideas that we're sharing!

**Earth Chorus**

## *Kids Can Make a World of Difference!*

This song is on Amazon Music, Apple Music, CD Baby and iTunes. It is also part of the album, *"Celebrate"*

**Earth Chorus**
(*sung*) One day in peace, one day in peace,
That's what we say, one day in peace.

(*spoken word*) Well, we're peace detectives and we know what to do,
Cause we're listening and living every peace clue.
So, I think it's time we all got together,
Put these peace clues in a letter.
Send it to people everywhere,
Tell them 'bout this dream that we all want to share …

**Earth Chorus**

(*spoken word*) The United Nations is an amazing place,
With leaders from many lands sitting face to face.
If we send them this letter and ask them to say …
That there *must* be peace for one little day

**Earth Chorus**

(*spoken word*) So, let's not waste any more time,
Let's write this letter in a cool rhyme.
Because kids can make a difference in their own way,
And we can have *a lot* to say …

**Earth Chorus**

(*sung*) We can make a difference if we try.

(*spoken*) Yeah!

## *Shake Your Own Hand*

**A Note to the Director:** There are two different versions of this song. *"The Friendship Song"* is a simplified version, found on the album, *"Songs That Make the Heart Feel Good."* A more sophisticated version is called, *"Shake Your Own Hand,"* found on the album, *"Celebrate."*

**"I'm an amazing person today!"**

**Earth Chorus**
Be your own best friend in the friendship song,
Shake your own hand and sing these words strong.
Look in the mirror, smile and say, "I'm an amazing person today!"
Yes, I'm an amazing person today!

Verse 1: Yes, you are your own best friend, you know.
Be good to yourself wherever you go.
Because peace begins inside of you …
With your thoughts, your words, with whatever you do. **(Earth Chorus)**

Verse 2: If someone says mean things and makes you feel sad,
Remember these words so you won't feel so bad.
It's a song that we'll sing to help you through,
When you don't know what to say or do. **(Earth Chorus)**

Verse 3: And if you get pushed while waiting in line,
Remember these words when you have that hard time.
It's a song that tells you you are great as you are.
You are your own shining star. **(Earth Chorus)**

Verse 4: If you ever get scared or kinda shy.
Or feel like you wanna cry and cry …
Just remember that you are the *best* you can be,
And sing this song once more with me! **(Earth Chorus)**

Verse 5: So always remember proudly hold your head high,
You're important, you're special, make your dreams fly!
Believe in yourself, be your own best friend,
With confidence and courage around every bend! **(Earth Chorus)**

I'm an amazing person … every minute, every hour, every second
Of every amazing day!

(*spoken word*) Remember that!

## *Wishes*

This song can be found on Amazon Music, Apple Music, CD Baby and on iTunes. It is on the album, *"Songs That Make the Heart Feel Good."*

**Earth Chorus**
Wishes, wishes,
These are my wishes for you, for you.
Wishes, wishes,
Make your own wishes come true.

Verse 1: May the sun shine upon you so sweetly,
May all your wishes come true.
May love fill your heart, right from the start
May joy fill your life every day.

**Earth Chorus**
Wishes, wishes,
These are my wishes for you, for you.
Wishes, wishes,
Make your own wishes come true.

Verse 2: May goodness and pleasure surround you.
May friends fill your life with joy.
May love fill your heart, right from the start,
May peace fill your life every day.

**Earth Chorus**
Wishes, wishes,
These are my wishes for you, for you.
Wishes, wishes,
Make your own wishes come true.

Verse 3: May fun and happiness soothe you,
May you feel the beauty of life!
May love fill your heart, right from the start,
May laughter fill live every day.

**Earth Chorus**
Wishes, wishes,
These are my wishes for you, for you.
Wishes, wishes,
Make your own wishes come true.

## *If You Have a Dream* (Bonus Song)

This song can be found on Amazon Music, Apple Music, CD Baby and iTunes. It is also part of the albums, *"Listen to the Whispers," "Lullabies of Love"* and *"Celebrate."*

(spoken word) Rise to your true self, who you really are!
Your life can be filled with unlimited possibilities. Reach for the stars.
You have the power to make your dreams come true.
The power is all inside you to dream, and to act upon your dreams.
To love, to find peace within you, and to be all of who you really are!
Stand fully in yourself. In your "I Am."
And look up High in all you do.

**Chorus**
If you have a dream, hold on to the dreamer,
Fill yourself up with music and light.
Reach out to your gifts that give you meaning,
Trust in your dream both day and night.

(Verse 1): Breathe in who you are, this dream is not far.
And trust in love to guide you.
Embrace what you feel you know to be real,
Look up high in all you do.

**Chorus**

(Verse 2) Protect your precious dream, allow it to be seen,
Don't let any darkness surround you.
Reach out with both wings, let your heart sing …
Look up high in all you do.

**Chorus**

## *"Peace Begins with You and Me"*

## Sheet Music

In addition to full musical notation of the theme song, *One Planet*, 6 bonus songs with full notation, piano accompaniment and lyrics are also included:

- *One Planet*
- *The No Bully Rap-Song*
- *You Can Change You*
- *Peace is a Verb*
- *Kids Can Make a World of Difference (aka One Day in Peace)*
- *Shake Your Own Hand*
- *If You Have a Dream*

To quickly and easily download the *"Peace Begins with You and Me"* script, director's guide, song lyrics and sheet music, please visit:

http://cherylmelody.com/peace-programs-adults/anti-bullying/peace-play-downloads/

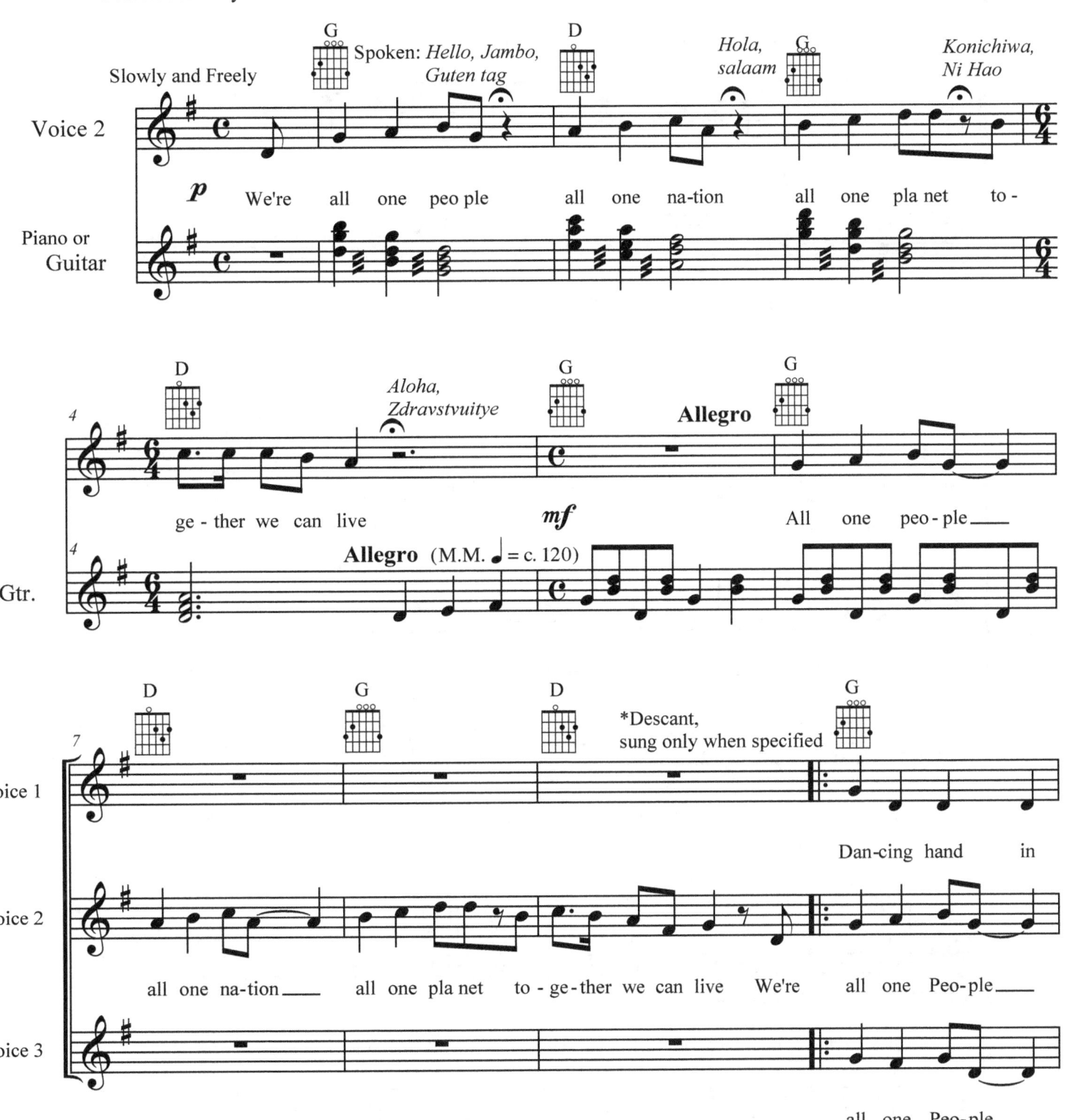

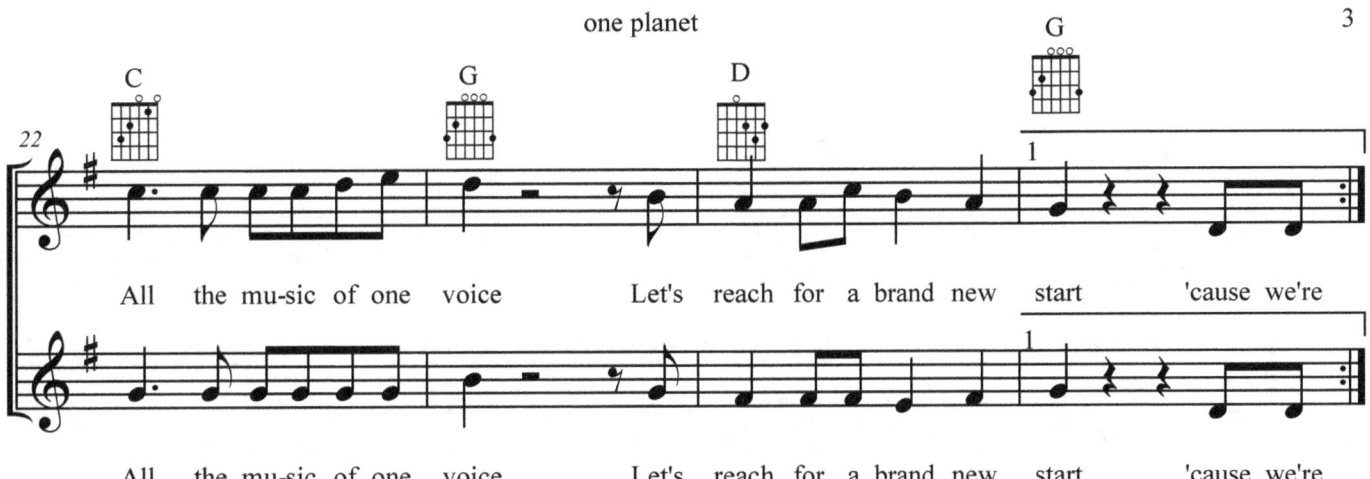
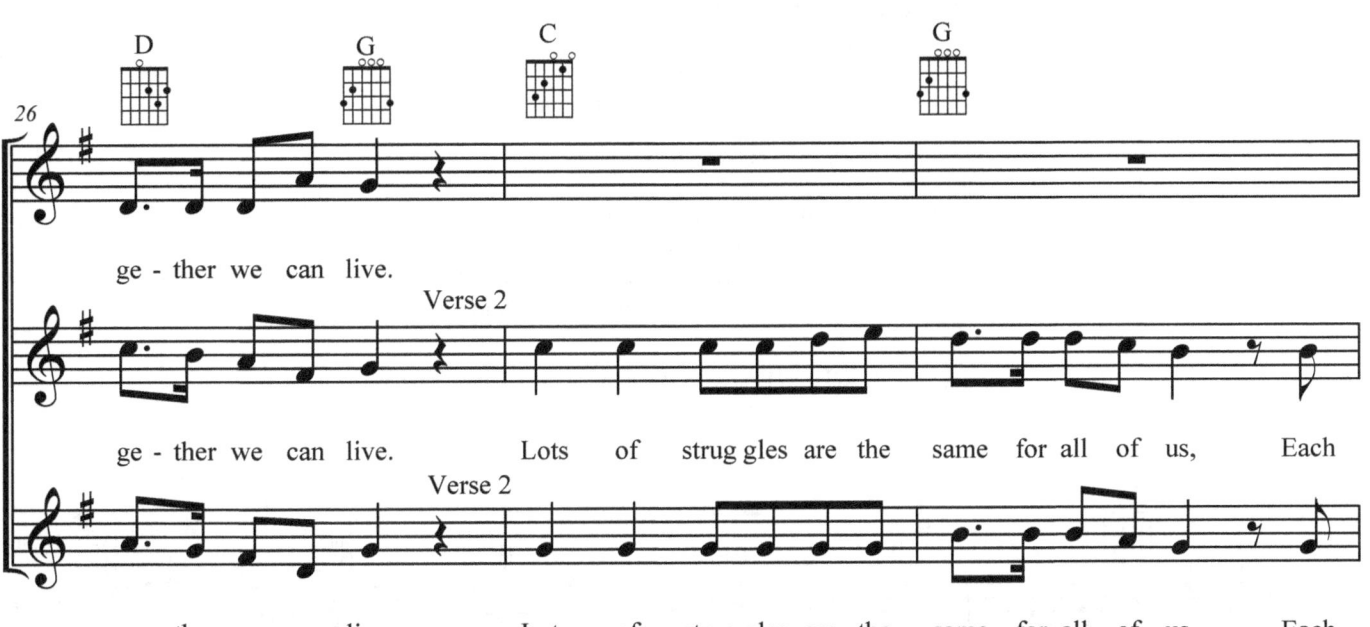
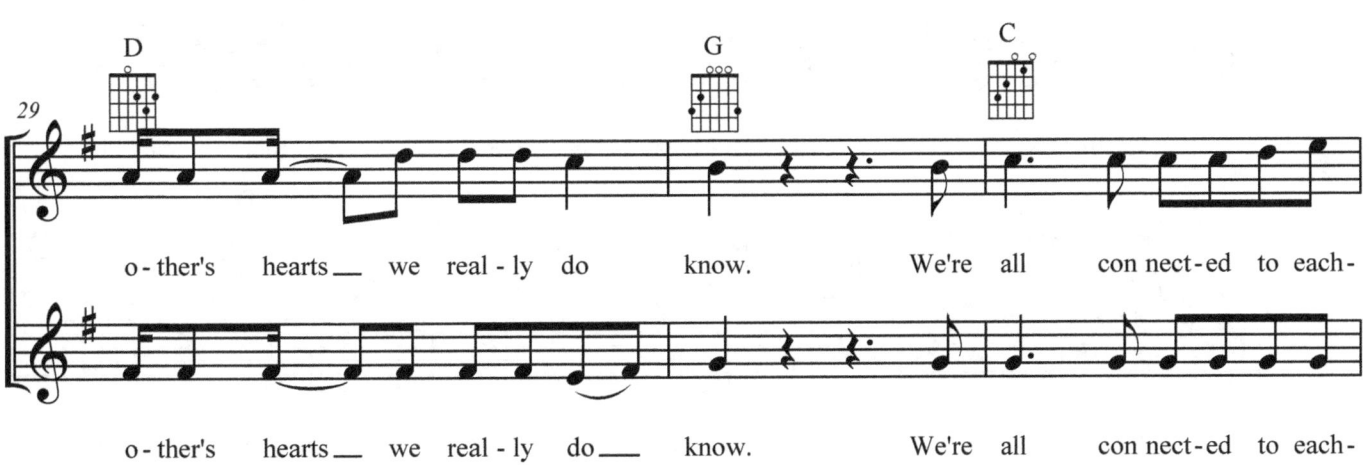

Verse 3: Show your kindness to each other,
Know that we are one.
There's magic in caring for another,
Your love shines like the sun.

CHORUS (no descant)

Verse 4: Sing this song to each other
Dance with joy hand in hand
We're everybody's sister and brother
So, strike up the one planet band

CHORUS with descant
CHORUS (no descant) to coda

Spoken: Heiwa, peace, peace, peace, Shalom, paz, sol, peace...peace

"ONE PLANET" Pronunciation Guide

| | |
|---|---|
| Jambo (Swahili "hello") | - JAM-bo |
| Guten Tag (German "good day") | - GOO-ten Tahk |
| Hola (Spanish "hello) | - oh-LAH |
| Salaam (Arabic "hello/goodbye/peace") | - sah-LAHM |
| Konichiwa (Japanese) | - ko-nee-chee-wah |
| Ni Hao (Chinese) | - nee-HOW |
| Aloha (Hawaiian "hello/goodbye") | - ah-LO-hah |
| Zdravstvuite (Russian) | - ZDRAV-ste-vwi-tye |
| | |
| Adios (Spanish "good bye") | - Ah-dee-YOS |
| Auf Weidersehen (German) | - owf VEE-der-sehn (closed e) |
| Shalom (Hebrew "hello/goodbye/peace") | - sha-LOM (closed o) |
| Tsai Chien (Chinese "good bye") | - tsai-CHIEN |
| | |
| Namaste (Sanskrit "The divine in me | - nah-mah-STAY |
|     Bows to the divine in you" (loosely translated) | |
| L'hitraot (Hebrew "see you soon") | - lih-hee-trah-OT (closed o) |
| Heiwa (Japanese "peace") | - hey-wah |
| Paz (Spanish "peace") | - Paz |
| Solh (Persian "peace") | - SOHL |

# No Bully Rap

Cheryl Melody

www.cherylmelody.com Cheryl Melody Productions ASCAP ©All Rights Reserved

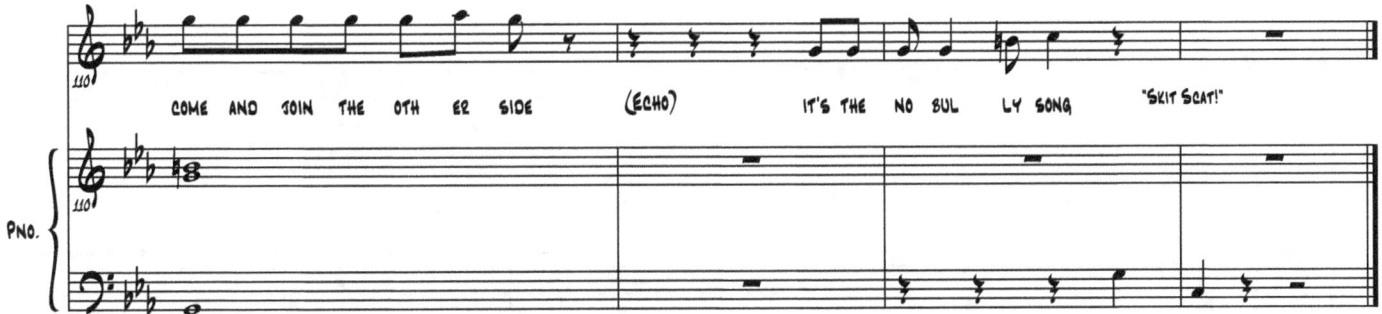

1. Partner Songs can be created of the "Skit Skat Dittin Dat" section and sung simultaneously with the "I've got feelings, you've got feelings section.

2. Partner songs can be created with the "I've got feelings, you've got feelings" section and sung simultaneously with "The nicer you are to yourself" section.

3. The last section can be sung 4 times, once with the bullying focus, once with the teasing focus, once with the gossiping focus, and the last time back to the bullying focus. Please hear the example of "The No Bully Rap" on the CD, "Celebrate!"

# You Can Change You

Cheryl Melody

Cheryl Melody Productions
http://www.cherylmelody.com
(c) All rights reserved

Cheryl Melody Productions
http://www.cherylmelody.com,
(c) All rights reserved

Peace is a Verb

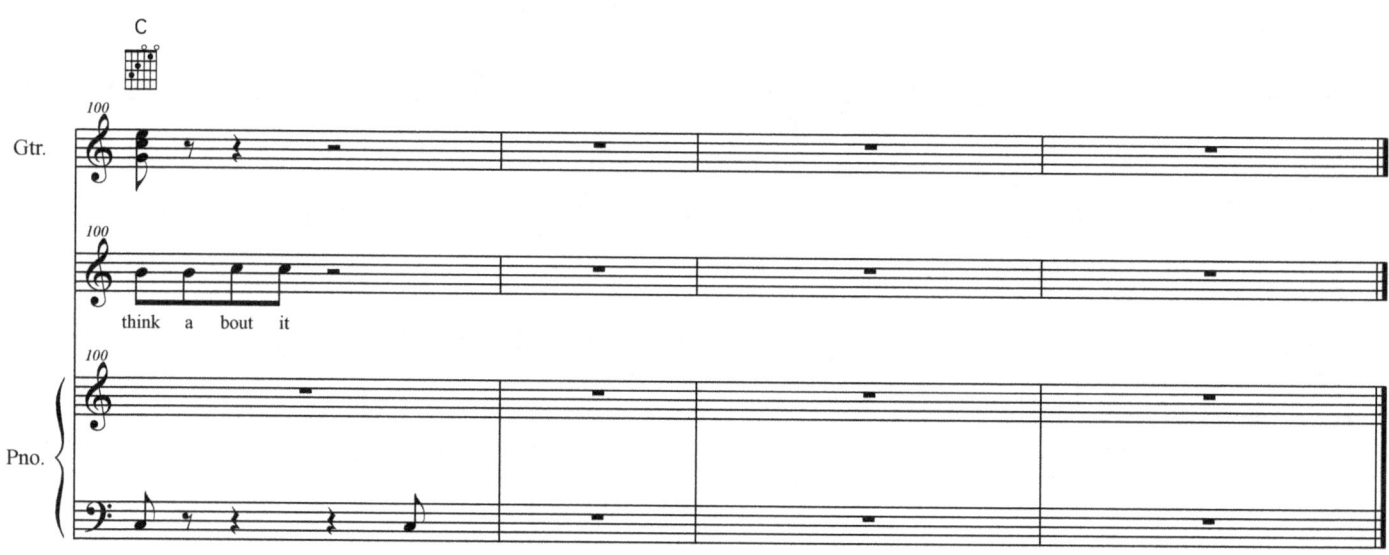

# Kids Can Make a World of Difference!

Cheryl Melody arr. S. Horowitz

♩ = 140

**Voice 1:** One day in peace___ One day in peace___ (tutti)
That's what we say,___ one day in peace. (Last time To Coda)

**Voice 2:** One day in peace___ One day in peace___ (tutti)
That's what we say,___ one day in peace. (Last time To Coda)

**Voice 3:** (Solo on first refrain only) One day in peace___ One day in peace___ (tutti)
That's what we say___ one day in peace. (one) (Last time To Coda)

Spoken (rap): Well we're peace de-tec-tives and we know what to do 'cuz we're listening and living eve-ry peace clue and I'm here to say that I've learned a lot___ a-bout

Cheryl Melody Productions
http://www.cherylmelody.com
(c) All rights reserved

**Verse 2 :**  Well I think its time we all got together
Put these peace clues in a letter
Send it to people everywhere
Tell them 'bout this dream that we all want to share

CHORUS

**Verse 3**  The United Nations is an amazing place
With leaders from many lands sitting face to face
If we send them this letter and ask them to say
That there MUST be peace for one little day.

CHORUS

**Verse 4**  So let's not waste anymore time
Let's write this letter in a cool rhyme
Cause kids can make a differece in their own way
And we can have a lot to say.

CHORUS to CODA

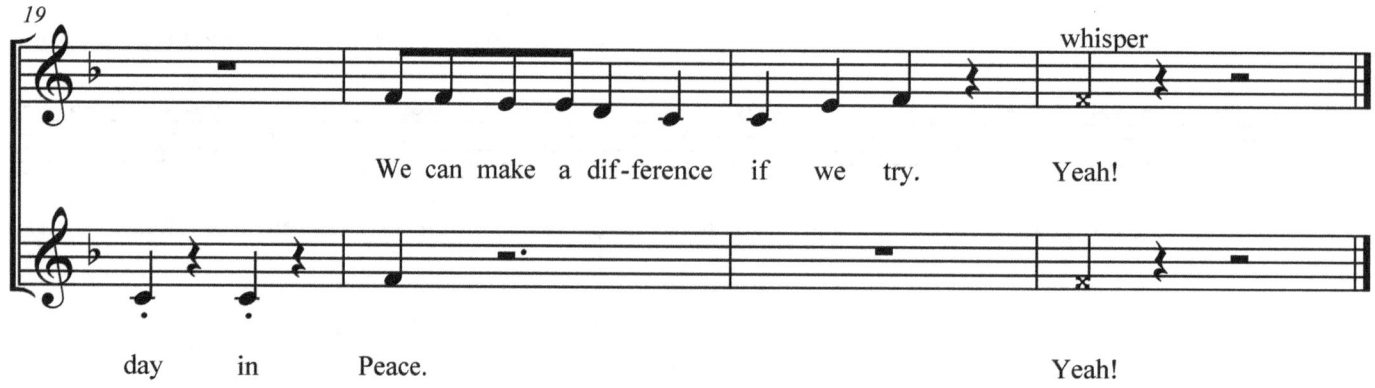

Cheryl Melody Productions
http://www.cherylmelody.com
(c) All rights reserved

# Shake Your Own Hand

**Cheryl Melody arr. S. Horowitz**

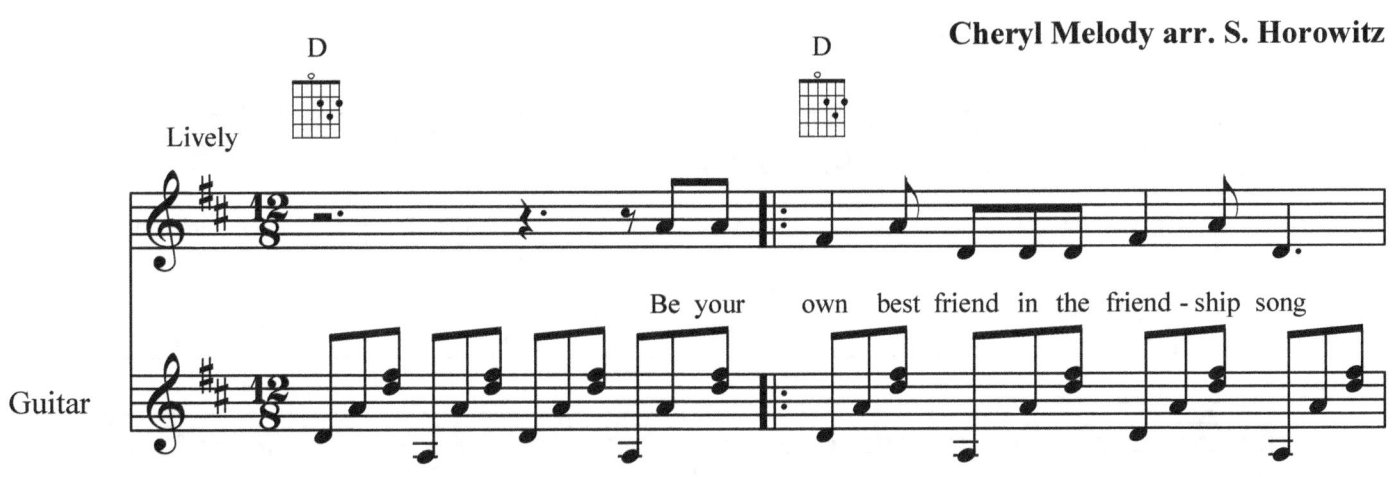

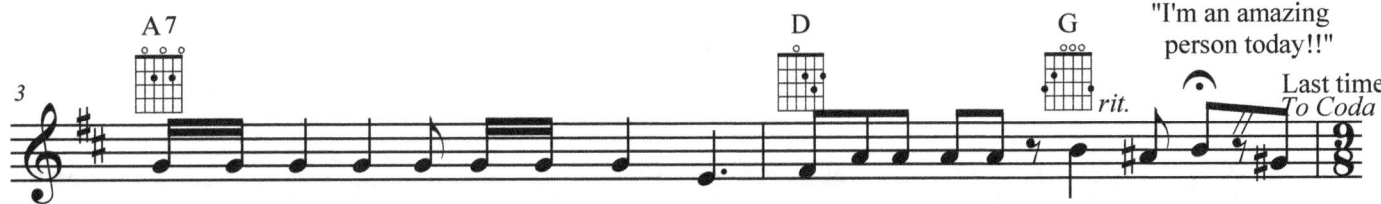

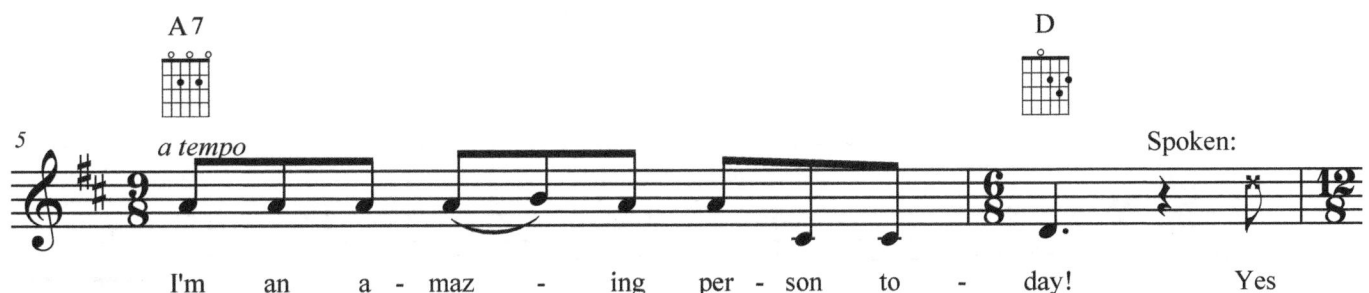

Cheryl Melody Productions www.cherylmelody.com
(c) All Rights Reserved

## "SHAKE YOUR OWN HAND" LYRICS
*(Starred \* lyrics are sung, please see score for corresponding melody.)*

CHORUS:  Be your own best friend in the friendship song,
Shake your own hand and sing these words strong.
Look in the mirror, smile, and say: "I'm an amazing person today!"
Yes I'm an amazing person today!

Verse 1:  Yes, you are your own best friend, you know,
Be good to yourself wherever you go,
'Cuz peace begins inside of you,
With your thoughts, your words, *with whatever you do. CHORUS

Verse 2:  Now if someone says rotten things and makes you feel kinda sad,
Just remember these words and you won't feel so bad,
It's a song that we'll sing to help you through,
*When you don't know what to say or do. CHORUS

Verse 3:  And if you get pushed while waiting in line,
Just remember these words when you have that hard time,
It's a song that tells you you're great as you are,
*You are your own shining star! CHORUS

Verse 4:  And if you ever get scared or kinda shy,
Or feel like you wanna cry and cry,
Just remember you are the best you can be,
*And sing the Friendship song once more with AMAZING little ol' me! CHORUS

Verse 5:  So always remember proudly hold your head high,
You're important, you're special, make your dreams fly.
Believe in yourself, be your own best friend,
With confidence and courage around every bend. CHORUS

Coda:  *I'm an amazing person, every minute, every hour, every second,
of every amazing day! Remember that!

# If You Have A Dream

**Cheryl Melody**

Cheryl Melody Productions
http://www.cherylmelody.com
(c) All Rights Reserved

# If You Have A Dream

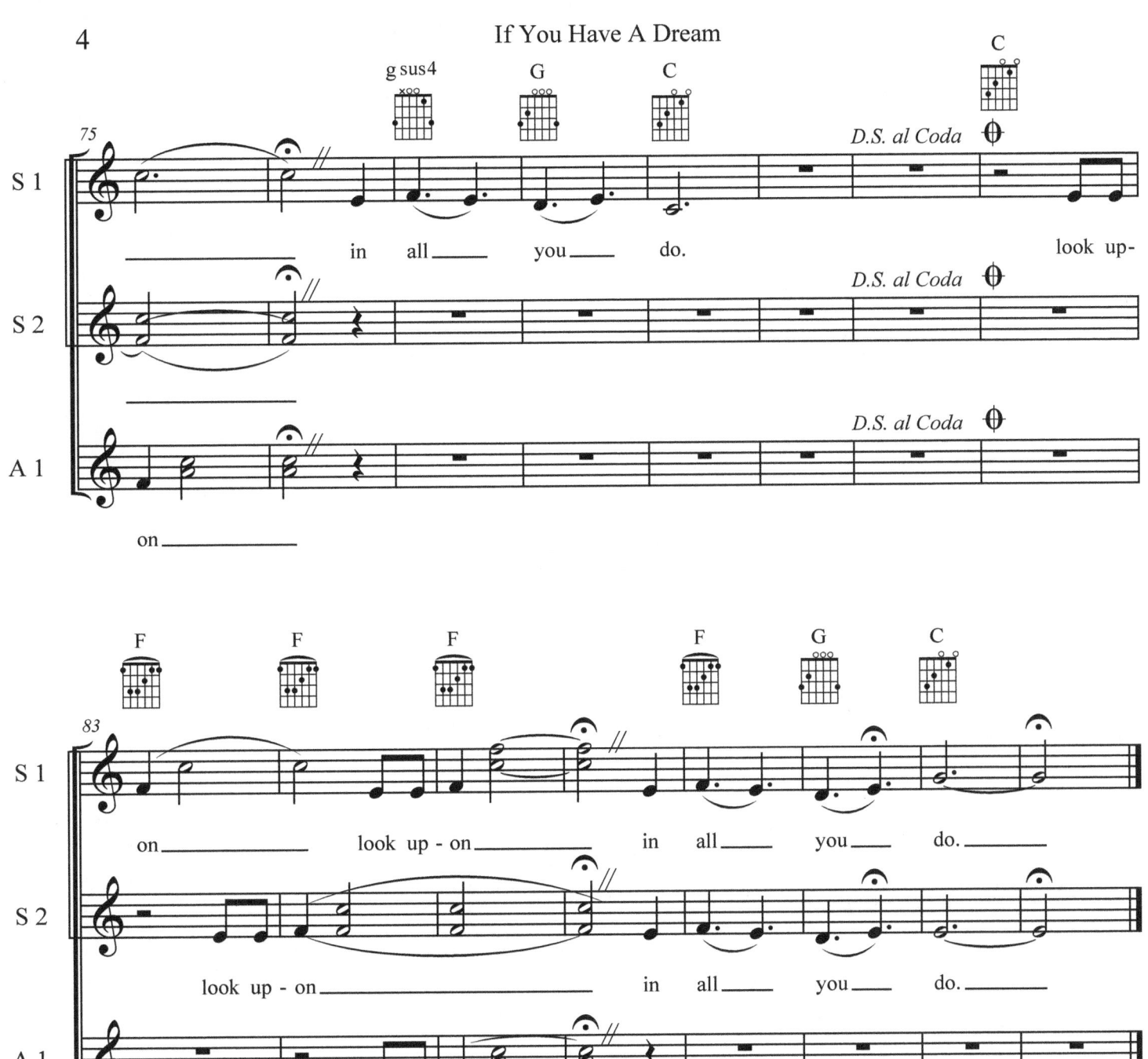

www.ingramcontent.com/pod-product-compliance
Lightning Source LLC
Chambersburg PA
CBHW081121080526
44587CB00021B/3689